# THE SUNDAY TIMES
# A LIFE IN THE DAY

# THE SUNDAY TIMES
# A LIFE IN THE DAY

Four decades of remarkable personalities from The Sunday Times Magazine

**TIMES BOOKS**
London

First published in 2003 by **Times Books**, an imprint of
**HarperCollins***Publishers*
77-85 Fulham Palace Road, Hammersmith, London W6 8JB
www.fireandwater.com

| 09 | 08 | 07 | 06 | 05 | 04 | 03 |
|----|----|----|----|----|----|----|
| 7  | 6  | 5  | 4  | 3  | 2  | 1  |

Editor: Hilary Stafford-Clark
Art Director: Linda Elander
Assistant Editor: Ria Higgins
Picture Editor: Suzanne Hodgart
Designer: Pia Constenius

A catalogue record for this book is
available from the British Library

ISBN 0 00 717253 2

Colour reproduction by Colourscan
Printed and bound in Great Britain by The Bath Press Ltd

# CONTENTS

# INTRODUCTION

**A Life in the Day** has become a journalistic legend. There have been many variations on it over the years in other publications, which have come and gone, but A Life in the Day's simple, straightforward format has turned into what must now be British journalism's longest-running weekly series.

The background, the inspiration, was commercial. In 1977 I was editor of The Sunday Times Magazine and the then editor of the paper, Harry Evans, was going on about the need for something at the back of the Mag. Readership research was showing that people thought the Mag was a waste of money – even though it was free – and was all about advertisements. In those days, the Mag did finish with about 20 consecutive pages of ads.

If I could come up with a regular, self-contained one-page editorial feature for the end of the Mag, it would leaven all the ads – and we could also charge more for the ad on the opposite page, calling it a "premium" ad.

We began a series called Home Town, in which well-known people were taken back to revisit the place where they grew up and to reminisce. I did the first one, with Edward Heath in Broadstairs, and very boring it was. After about six weeks, I chucked it. It was so hard to keep quality control. You might have a well-known name, but that did not guarantee it was going to be interesting. Then we had an opinion column called Sacred Cows, attacking popular beliefs or institutions. This was written by writers, so in theory the writing would always be good, but the problem was tone – it turned out to be a bit of a moan, really.

I then thought back to a column I had done as a student, 20 years earlier, when I was editor of Palatinate, the Durham University student paper. Each week we did a diary of a day in the life of a boat-club hearty, a theology don, a science student, or whatever. All made up by me. Poking fun. I called it A Life in the Day, the reverse of the old clichéd phrase.

I suggested we did a series on real lives, famous and non-famous people, but concentrating only on the non-working part of their day: the mundane, domestic, trivial – the stuff we can all identify with, such as what time do you get up, do you have tea or coffee, do you leave your clothes out the night before?

Boring, boring, said several people. So I tried out the idea over an office lunch, going round the table, asking people about their non-working day. I started with Patrick Nicholson, the chief sub. When it came to his choice of clothes for each new day, he replied: "I consult my diary." As far as I had been aware, Patrick always wore the same sort of suit, clean shirt, neat tie. Nothing outrageous or even unusual. So why did he check his diary? It turned out he always kept a note on exactly what he wore to work each day, and made sure that nothing was repeated over a two-week spell.

That was it. If Patrick had this little ritual no one knew about, imagine what gems we might dig out of Famous People.

When I left the Mag, about a year later, I did Guy the Gorilla as a Life in the Day – the first "made-up" one we had done. I did actually go to London Zoo, spent some hours with Guy and his keeper, and got as much real information as possible, but it was a joke to myself, reminding me of my Durham days. I thought it would be the last Life in the Day – the next editor would be bound to chuck it and start a new series. But blow me, it's going as strongly as ever.

A Life in the Day is still on one page, with one simple photo, self-contained, easy to read, yet with an inbuilt narrative leading you on. With famous people, you don't have to ask them about their famousness – most readers already know about that. What they don't know about are the ordinary parts of their day. The format also fits unknown people – which comes as a relief in this age when so many columns and papers are celeb-dominated. And the title itself is even better than I first imagined. Inside each day, we all do have several lives.

So far, around 1,250 people have described their lives in the column, covering 70 nationalities, from heads of state to bag ladies. It's become a national institution.

In my long and awfully exciting working life, I have published 40 books and produced about four million words of journalism. But I fear – sorry suspect... what am I saying? I'm proud to think that A Life in the Day might well be my best-remembered thing.

**Hunter Davies**
**Editor of The Sunday Times Magazine 1975-77**

70s

And then who turns up on Copacabana Beach but Slipper of the Yard? Not at all what Biggsie had in mind
**RONNIE BIGGS, GREAT TRAIN ROBBER**

# RONALD BIGGS
## MAY 21, 1978

Ronnie Biggs, 48 (known to his neighbours as Mike Haynes), great train robber and fugitive, lives with his son, Mike, 2, in Sepetiba, Rio de Janeiro, where he was photographed by Lord Snowdon.

**I had to** give up the maid three years ago – simply couldn't afford her, old chap, you know how it is – so I spend a lot of the day pottering round the villa. I do all the cleaning and washing. The craziest thing is that I'm not allowed to work. As a young crook in England they were always telling me to work. Now I want to, they won't let me. There's always something on. We seem to be on the tourist circuit. Just before you arrived, two landladies from Blackpool came to pay their respects, said coming to Brazil and not seeing Biggsie was like going to Egypt and not seeing the pyramids. And of course Slipper of the Yard came four years ago, to arrest me. I was at my lowest. I was missing Charmian [his wife] and the kids. I was tired of running. The money was long gone. I thought if I gave myself up and said, "Okay, it's me, folks!" they'd take it into account. So I got a friend to fix a deal with the Express. Thirty-five grand. I was all fired up and ready to go, and who turns up on Copacabana Beach? Slipper of the Yard. Now that wasn't what Biggsie had in mind at all. I wanted to go back, sure, but as the guy who'd done the decent. Not hauled back in cuffs like a screaming felon.

The morning they came for me, my bird, Raimunda, told me she was pregnant. Most days that would have made an impression. But I found myself in a cell, feeling very sour, with a couple of Rio taxi drivers. There I am, all upset, and one of these blokes says to me: "If you could pretend to have got a Brazilian girl pregnant, bribe or beg one, anything, but get one, they can't extradite you." I said: "Look, fellas, you won't believe this, but…"

I don't see myself getting back to Britain. And I don't believe I'll ever go to prison again. Why put me back in prison, in a criminal environment, when I've been straight so long? What do they want to do – make a criminal out of me? **In 2001, Biggs returned to the UK to complete his 30-year sentence, and wed Raimunda in 2002. A series of strokes has left him paralysed.**

# FIONA RICHMOND
## DECEMBER 2, 1978

**Fiona Richmond, 32, having achieved fame as a sex symbol, now describes herself as an actress and a journalist. After years of 'road testing' men, she says she has settled down with one bloke.**

**If I've been** on stage or doing some late-night radio chat show about sex, I'll sleep in. There's no typical routine, except when I'm writing one of my books or my Men Only column. On those days I never bother to get properly dressed. I'll lie around in just a man's shirt, scribbling away or dictating to a friend who's very fast on the typewriter. He works for the Gay News and bristles a bit when I make jokes about coons or fairies. He knows I'm not serious. People think writing about sex is a doddle but it's actually incredibly hard. Vocabulary's the main problem; it's difficult not to repeat yourself. The ideas come easily. After all, I've done the research – deary me, makes me tired to even think about it. But it may have made it easier for me to settle down with one bloke, like now. I can't understand how a woman can marry the first man she's slept with. After all, you don't drive a car without taking lessons first, do you? But I'm basically monogamous. Faithful to one guy completely, whether it's for five minutes or five years.

# People think being a sex symbol's just lying around without your clothes on

Driving was my main hobby. I used to race round Brands Hatch a lot until they wouldn't insure me for shows any more. And I got rid of my FU2 numberplate. I got bored with people knowing where I was all the time. People think being a sex symbol is just lying around without clothes on. Actually it's exhausting. I enjoy opening shops. I'll declare the shop open, then do 10 minutes of mildly rude repartee with the crowd before we let them in. I've never had any real trouble with men. They want to kiss me, so I do get lips landing all over my face, but I'm used to that.

If my friend is out during the day, I'll plan something special for when he comes back. He'll be home earlier if he thinks he'll find me naked on the fridge or something. Sometimes I'll dress up in black corsets and boots and tie him to the rocking chair. People imagine me waltzing round the fleshpots, all thighs, big knockers and trouble, but they're quite wrong. I'm a real homebody.

**Married in 1983, divorced in 1998, Fiona has a daughter. Her Hampshire b&b, The Onion Store (designed as a 'lovers' retreat') is proving irresistible. She also has a hotel, the Petit Bacaye Cottage, on the island of Grenada.**

# GUY THE GORILLA

## DECEMBER 4, 1977

**Guy the Gorilla, 31, is the oldest gorilla in Europe. His chest is thought to measure around 7ft. He lives in a three-room cage at London Zoo, where he is looked after by George Callard, head keeper of apes.**

**I always wake** at dawn but I do nothing about it. There's a very flash chimp nearby called Sidney who's always making a noise first thing, but I ignore him. They snore as well, the chimps, but not as bad as the orangs. I ignore them all. I just lie and wait for George. Why should I hurry?

If it's not George but some other keeper, I might give him a look, perhaps go across to the wire and try to get him, just to show who's boss. But it's usually George. I catch his eye, then I look away again, then I dart him another look. I don't go in for all this friendship stuff with human beings, not like those stupid chimps. They'll talk to everybody.

I've got three cages — my back den where I sleep, my show cage and the outside cage. Nobody's got a bigger cage. I might not be the oldest gorilla in the world — though I'm the oldest in Europe. I might not be the biggest. But I am the greatest.

At 9 o'clock George opens the sliding doors and I go into my show cage for breakfast. It's always the same old stuff — a large bowl of Cooper's pellets. Monkey chow, so George calls it. They're scattered all over the floor and I have to scratch around to pick them up. Very undignified. I get 800 grams every morning and Lomie gets 700.

I hoped you wouldn't ask about Lomie. Okay, she's a lady gorilla. She has her own back den but we share the rest of the quarters. She came here in 1969, I think it was. I'd been on my own for 20 years. If you ask me, it was PR. They wanted a Mating in the Zoo and a Baby Gorilla. She was quite good fun at first, Lomie, when she came. Well, it made a change. We had a bit of a wrestle, bit of a punch-up, just to show her who was boss. No, we never mated. Do you have to go into all this? I know disgusting rumours are going round this place about me. I heard George tell somebody I was impotent. And that stupid chimp Sidney asked me when I was "coming out". I just don't fancy her. That's all. It didn't bother me when she had her affair last year with that jerk from Bristol Zoo, some over-sexed cheap-jack gorilla called Samson. She came back and had a baby. That kept the PR men happy.

I spend most of the morning munching my disgusting breakfast. Lomie nicks most of it. I can't work up the energy. But it gives me something to do instead of watching the stupid humans. You wouldn't believe the cretinous remarks I have to put up with. "Look, it's King Kong." "Ooh, isn't he like our Dad." The afternoon's the worst, especially on Sundays and Bank Holidays. It's standing room only for miles around. I deliberately sit still, doing absolutely nothing for up to an hour, just to teach them. Then when I move, they all shriek. There are some nice humans. Where's that postcard? Mr and Mrs

## Stupid humans. I'll sit still for an hour, just to teach them. And when I move, they shriek

Heaton, that's it. He's a retired master plumber from near Leeds. I get cards all the time, and on my birthday. They've come regular for years, spend every day of their holidays here, just to see me. Ask George.

I can remember the day in 1968 when they banned the public from feeding the animals. I used to get through up to 20 ice-cream cartons a day, plus as many sweets as I could grab, and then, overnight, wham, it all stopped. I lay down in my cage for three days and moaned.

Closing time's the best part of the day. That's when I get the real food. Tonight, let's see, George says I'm getting six bananas, one pear, four apples, two tomatoes, half a cucumber, bunch of grapes, slice of cabbage, a lettuce and a packet of dates. And two pints of milk. I always sit up to eat that pellet stuff in the morning, but at night I lie leaning on one elbow on my straw. George says I look like a Roman. If I want to get really comfy I'll lie flat on my stomach. It's a pretty draggy life being cooped up here all day.

I don't get bothered at night, not since they put Lomie in her own cage. We don't sleep together, thank God. I eat in peace and quiet and then it's heads down, and I'm off.

**Guy died of a heart attack after having a tooth extracted in 1978. His statue can be seen at the Zoo.**

# JIMMY SAVILE

## JULY 16, 1978

**Jimmy Savile, OBE, 51, started his working life as a coalminer in Yorkshire, joined the BBC as a DJ in the late 1960s and now presents Jim'll Fix It and Top of the Pops. He has raised over £3m for charity.**

**I seldom sleep** in the same bed two nights running. I've got five flats, in London, Leeds, Bournemouth and Scarborough, a caravan in Dorset and the use of rooms in Broadmoor and Stoke Mandeville Hospitals [he is assistant entertainments officer at Broadmoor, entertainments officer at Stoke Mandeville]. Today I surfaced sometime after 10am in my London flat just round the corner from Broadcasting House. Breakfast is whatever I can find in the kitchen. Today it was a piece of cheese a fortnight old and a packet of biscuits. Dress is nearly always a tracksuit and training shoes. Round my neck I wear a 22-carat medallion depicting the Leeds coat of arms. It gives me the freedom of all the public toilets in the city. Twelve noon and the door-bell rings. It's one of my honorary personal assistants, here to drive me to the Grosvenor House Hotel where I'm a guest at a Variety Club of Great Britain luncheon, sitting between Lord Mountbatten and Sir Billy Butlin. I'm there to present the Variety Club with a cheque for £1,001.49, which I raised in a sponsored 82-mile jog and walk from Trafalgar Square to Eastbourne [where he collected his latest car, a £46,000 Rolls]. I telephone Charles Hullighan, administrator of portering at Leeds Infirmary [where Jimmy is a porter] and another honorary assistant. He brings me up to date. Then I make for studio S2 across the road to record Jim'll Fix It. On the way I get waylaid by four teenage girls seeking autographs. Two elderly ladies step forward to greet me. I give them each a kiss. They promise me their undying love.

Within half an hour it's all on tape, which gives me just enough time to ring through the copy for my weekly column in a national newspaper. Then a taxi whisks me off to Shepherd's Bush for Top of the Pops. The driver wants an autograph for his kids. I oblige, as usual. In my dressing room, I sink into a chair and light up a Havana. Because of a technical hitch the recording is very slow. But by 9.30 everything's in the can. After signing numerous autographs, just after 10pm, we split. I leave with a record company executive who's seeking advice.

My gold medallion depicts the Leeds coat of arms. It gives me the freedom of all the city's public toilets

# DIANE HARPWOOD

## MAY 7, 1978

**Diane Harpwood, 33, a housewife, lives in Halifax with her husband, Ben, an engineering-works manager, and their small children, Jodi and Ben.**

**I start my** day the Valium way at 7.20am when my departing husband brings me a mug of tea and a diazepam tablet. A Valium a day keeps the psychiatrists at bay.

My two children burst into the bedroom yelling, shouting, bawling. They've been up since 6, full of joie de vivre. Can they be mine? I go a few rounds with Ben, the youngest, who's nearly two. He wants my tea, but I must have it. I know it's unfair – he should pick on someone his own size. I drive them out screaming like a banshee and heaping curses on their beautiful, innocent little heads like a hag from Macbeth.

Breakfast time. I am exhausted, bad-tempered – drained of patience. Yes, already. Another day of soul-destroying solitude looms ahead. A dehumanising repetition of a detestable routine. I hurtle around the kitchen from frying pan to fridge and back again. I loathe, I hate, I abhor housework – nevertheless that's what I do next. Only trendy, middle-class lady journalists like Jilly Cooper can get away with having mucky houses. Not that they want to; quite the reverse in fact. Have you noticed how it's a compulsion with them to boast about how the cat was sick in

## I drive the children out, heaping curses like a hag from Macbeth

the boeuf bourguignon? Or how they failed to notice that the stripped-pine dresser – picked up at a junk shop for £15 – was feet thick in dust until friends wrote rude words on it with their fingers? Down here in Working-class Land you'd be excommunicated for far less than that. Among us lower orders cleanliness isn't next to godliness: they are one and the same thing. We wouldn't know we were poor if we didn't read the adverts in The Sunday Times – the only newspaper we buy. They leave us gasping. We regard our monetary malaise as a temporary condition brought on by inflation and curable in time. If we didn't, we'd go insane. Bedtime is 9.30-10pm. Normally with a library book, occasionally with my husband.

**After Diane's Life in the Day appeared, Virago published her book, Tea and Tranquillisers: The Diary of a Happy Housewife. She went on to publish two more books and recently retired to live in Spain with her husband.**

I offer him advice if he feeds me. The deal is on. We head for the Lotus House in Edgware Road. I start at the top of the menu and work down till I'm full. I'm just a dustbin. My day usually ends when everybody around me has flaked out and dispersed. It's about 2am before I climb into my four–poster with a mug of tea and my favourite bedtime reading – New Scientist. Usually I book an alarm call. But not tonight. I gave my telephone number to a girl on TOTP who said she wanted to talk to me. I asked her to ring me up at 9am tomorrow. That way I save the cost of a call and start on the credit side. **Jim was knighted in 1990. He Fixed It for the last time in 1994.**

# TOM BAKER

## SEPTEMBER 17, 1978

**Tom Baker, 44, spent six years as a monk but left after deciding it was time for 'pubs and women' and went on to become TV's favourite Dr Who. He likes to travel light (note the toothbrush in his top pocket).**

**You could say** yesterday was fairly typical of a day in my life when we're not recording Dr Who. I woke up at 5.15am in a brown cork-lined room in Soho and then got into bed. But where am I? I dreamt about a tall, thin woman, but who is she? I suffer recurring images of tall, skinny ladies. They look so good and release all those fantasies. I woke up again at 6.10am. I got up and began the process of dragging my feet to their final destination at night. I was hit by terrible waves of anxiety. The feeling of loneliness that smacks of self-pity. I drank a glass of water and felt for a toothbrush, wondering where on earth I was. If I'd had a radio I would have put it on, but it's too early, of course, for Radio 3.

The anxiety persisted and I thought: "Suicide is the answer." I got out of bed and looked at some electrical flex. The ceiling was too low. How could I have hanged myself in a room only 5ft 10in high?

Then I took a sly bath and checked my pockets. I found £114 and a pair of clean underpants and began to walk confidently. All you really need for confidence is always to have a toothbrush and a hundred or two in your pocket. Oh, and a chequebook. I'm very check conscious. I usually dress in check trousers containing a cheque book. That and a velvet jacket and a raincoat. I went out and bought The Times and read the obituaries. There was no pleasure in them for me.

At 9.30am it was voiceover time at a Soho recording studio. I performed for Norsca Foam Baths and they seemed pleased by my enthusiasm. Afterwards I signed an autograph for a child called Donalbain and a few minutes later I signed one for a child called Wee Peng. Then I went for a drink. I usually go to the Swiss Tavern, the Carlisle Arms, the Coach and Horses or the Yorkminster. After a few drinks the miracle is that one has something to say. Then I feel an obligation to feel no anxiety because of being recognised. There is a constant stream of hellos, nods and autographs. All very good medicine for anxiety.

At midday I went to the Yorkminster, hoping for the miracle that I might see someone I'd never seen before. After lunch in the Paparazzi – I usually eat the calf's liver and bacon – I went to a rehearsal for the BBC in North Acton. It's Kafkaville. At teatime I arrived at The Colony Room and Francis Bacon bought me a large gin and tonic. The anxieties went away and the conviction grew that I had something to say on any subject. Kenny Clayton played the piano and a bunch of inebriates harmonised to Home on the Range.

I went back to the Yorkminster in the hope of finding some conversation before bedlam set in. Then I went to Gerry's Club and met Peter Crouch, the agent, and played

## I went to the Yorkminster, hoping for the miracle that I might see someone I had never seen before

some pool and lost. Dee Lynch, the manageress, embraced me and that was nice. Then I talked about cancer for a while with a man who had a bad cough. After that I was introduced to a Welsh schoolteacher, who said he was delighted to meet me. We shook hands and he promptly had a heart attack. Astonishingly enough, there were two doctors in the house – well, three if you include me – and the poor man was carried out and put into an ambulance. And then we embarked on a conversation about having heart attacks.

I tottered off back to Gerry's Club and had several nightcaps and felt relieved that another day had passed. As usual there was someone there with whom to discuss crumpet and the meaning of life. I then popped into Ronnie Scott's club and sat there at the bar self-consciously affecting a knowledge of jazz that I haven't got. Then I went back to Gerry's for another drink, and after I'd cadged a Valium from someone I went home to my padded cell.

**Tom played the doctor until 1981. In 1980 he married Lalla Ward, his co-star. After parting from her 'quite passionately', he wed the director Sue Jerrard in 1987.**

# MARY PHILPOTT

## OCTOBER 8, 1978

**Mary Philpott, 55, left her job in personnel in 1953 to care for her mother and father, who have since died. Describing herself as 'a derelict', she lives in Wallington. Mary wrote her own Life in the Day.**

**I am totally** alone, except for my cat, Tosca, who, like me, is one of today's rejects. She was thrown out by her previous owners and made her way to me. She is old, and swears and spits occasionally, more from habit than anger, and this I understand. She too has a reason to feel bitter, and she and I recognise kindred spirits and get on very well. My day begins at 7.30am, when I feed Tosca and have my breakfast, which invariably consists of two cups of tea. Later I go to the shops, where I buy a tin of cat food and, if I can afford it, a tin of vegetable soup for my own dinner. I've been virtually penniless since my father died two years ago. My mother, whom I loved dearly, died in 1968. I still mourn her. For a few months the social security office in Sutton allowed me a small sum to cover my rates, heating, etc, but this was stopped by the Dickensian officials, who, in their infinite wisdom, decided I had not made enough effort to get a job. Unfortunately, it had not occurred to these latter-day Bumbles that a woman of 55, with no recent experience, had very slight chance indeed to get work, particularly in view of the unemployment prevailing at the moment.

In the afternoon I go to my library. In the winter it is warm there, and in the summer it is a place to go, a transient escape. I've had no holiday since 1961, and I like to look at travel books, and dream. They are very understanding, not to say tolerant, in there and if they ever get tired of the sight of me, poring over their books, they are too tactful to show any displeasure. But quite possibly, since I am an anonymous figure, they do not notice me.

I'm not a great conversationalist, which is fortunate for me, for from the time I get up until I retire thankfully to bed, I doubt if I say more than half a dozen words to anyone. I've no friends, and there is just no point in talking, anyway. Some years ago I was able to buy myself a record player, and this I've hung onto grimly, although almost all my other possessions have been sold. My evenings are usually spent in the company of Mozart's Third Violin Concerto, and Dvorak's New World Symphony, which never fails to make me weep.

I sit and type little efforts like this partly to assuage the dreadful monotony and poverty of my existence

# BARBARA CARTLAND

MAY 28, 1978

**Barbara Cartland, 76, has sold over 80 million copies of her romantic novels. She lives near Hatfield and has two sons and one daughter.**

**I wake up** at 8am when the gardener buzzes me so he can take Duke, the black Labrador, out. He is one of the Queen's Sandringham strain and always stays in my room at night. The Pekinese, Twi-Twi, sleeps at the end of my four-poster. My old maid, Purcell, who has been with me 33 years and is now in her 80s, comes in about 8.45 with breakfast, which Reeves, the butler, has carried upstairs for her. I get up, do my hair and put on make-up – I like looking nice and I believe in self-discipline. And I don't mind admitting I wear false eyelashes. I eat the same thing for breakfast every day: an egg, my bran – I'm a great believer in bran – a tablespoon of honey and ginseng tea. And 70 or 80 vitamin pills. I read six newspapers. I answer all my letters when Mrs Waller, my chief private secretary, arrives at 9. We deal with phone calls and any urgent things: today it was doing the week's menus with the chef. Really, the mornings here are like a bad Noël Coward play. Telephones, secretaries and dogs all demanding attention. My maid organises what I wear and my hairdresser comes in several times a week. I wear a lot of what Sir Norman Hartnell calls Cartland Pink. It is a warm,

## Pink is a happy colour. Beige makes a woman look like a baked potato

happy colour when you get old. I hate beiges, they make a woman look like a baked potato.

At 12.45 I shut myself away with Mrs Elliott. I dictate or write between 6,000 and 9,000 words by 3.30, lying on the sofa. Towards the end of a chapter I ask Mrs Elliott: "How many words?" The dogs recognise the sentence and immediately jump up, and we go for a walk through the garden. We have tea at 4pm – usually a biscuit and some cake. Then I work through until 7 researching. I have a hot bath – two hot water bottles put in my bed – and I retire after putting on my FF cream and putting in my Lady Jane flat curlers. I go to sleep about 10.30. Yes, I work very hard, but what else does someone of my age do? With four permanent and six subsidiary secretaries, two dogs, a house and estate to run, I just keep working.

**Barbara Cartland was created a DBE in 1991. She died in 2000, at 98. She was then the world's best-selling author.**

My other indulgence is my treasured typewriter, an ancient Royal model I found languishing in a junk shop. I bought it, lovingly cleaned, oiled and refurbished it. Thus I can sit and type little efforts like this, partly to assuage the dreadful monotony and poverty of my existence, and partly to convince myself I'm not really on the scrapheap. Most probably, though, I set this down so there will be some record that I exist at all. I doubt it myself. **After Mary's Life in the Day, the Magazine received its biggest-ever response from readers; an American professor wrote to tell her she was a born writer. But her life remained much the same and she died of a heart attack in 2001.**

# MICHAEL HESELTINE

## DECEMBER 11, 1977

**Michael Heseltine, 44, Conservative MP for Henley, was born in Swansea and went to Pembroke College, Oxford. He lives in Banbury with his wife, Anne, and children Annabel, 14, Alexandra, 11, and Rupert, 10.**

**The alarm goes** at 7.30. It's on my wife's side of the bed. I'm not much good in the early morning. I can't be alert and switched on before I've even got up. Once the Today programme called and asked for a reply to somebody who had been particularly vitriolic about one of my speeches. But I didn't know what he'd said. My radio wasn't working, so there was nothing for it except to go out to the garage on a very frosty morning and turn on the car radio to hear on the next news bulletin what had been said about me. But if you're a politician you come to expect this sort of thing.

Breakfast is at 8am. I bring my wife breakfast in bed – sometimes; not something I would wish to make a habit. But scrambled eggs is something at which I can hold my own with anybody. The family's lives all diverge at breakfast and, when Parliament is sitting, we may not come together again until breakfast next morning. The thing I miss in life more than anything is that I don't have more time to do things with my children. But every three weeks it's Heseltine's turn to do the school run. Taking the children to school means I have a whole 15 minutes with them.

Clothes don't interest me much. In the morning I fumble into the cupboard to find something suitable. I know vaguely that you don't wear brown ties with blue shirts, but I'm not a sophisticated dresser. When I need a new suit my tailor of 20 years, Mr Neillson of Savile Row, comes to my office with a measuring tape and patterns. A suit emerges in due course. I don't know why my hair gives other people so much bother. I get it cut on quarter days, usually. I don't have a special hairdresser – heavens, no! Just where I happen to be. A very nice, efficient lady did it at London Airport the other day. I tend to get it cut at airports; it fills in the time I have spare.

It's an 80-mile journey from Banbury, and I commute every day by car, unless Parliament is sitting late. My car is a 1977 Daimler Sovereign. Until yesterday I'd had a Jaguar for seven years, a marvellous car: it did 82,000 miles and gave little trouble, and I only switched to the Daimler because they gave up making the type of Jaguar I liked. I've got a permanent parking arrangement at a car park a block from the office. But I regularly walk from my office to the House of Commons, not because I think I ought to for exercise, but because I love to walk.

This morning I received 26 invitations to lunch. I never accept an invitation where the meal offered is a quick snack. If I did I would be wilting at my office desk halfway through the afternoon. I must have proper food, a hot meal with good ingredients and well cooked. Cold food is not a proper meal. I run through most of the

## I get my hair cut on quarter days. I don't have a special hairdresser – heavens, no!

national daily newspapers, starting with The Times at breakfast. I think it has the most balanced, factual coverage. The Telegraph has the most news. But most of the people I meet, whether in business or politics, if they mention newspapers never mention a political story. I'm always struck by how small a part politics plays in people's lives. I'm not a great reader of books; there are a lot of government reports I have to read. In the time left I prefer to do other things like gardening, or photographing birds. During the last recess I hacked away at a shrubbery, I don't think a thing had been done with it in 20 years.

When the House of Commons is not sitting I get home between 7.30 and 8. I like to put on jeans, a sweater and slippers as soon as I get in. I don't fix a stiff drink or any other sort. I prefer to wait for dinner, when we have wine. Normally we've got somebody to do the cooking, but when we haven't, Anne cooks and I stack the dishwasher. We're out a couple of nights a week to dinner – it's a matter of great regret that so many of our friends can no longer afford to give dinner parties the way they used to. It's such an agreeable way to end the day.

**Michael Heseltine went on to hold several ministerial posts, including that of deputy prime minister. He suffered a heart attack in 1993 and was created a life peer in 2001.**

# LUCIANO PAVAROTTI

## SEPTEMBER 3, 1978

**Luciano Pavarotti, 42, was born in Modena, Italy, and has sung in leading opera houses all around the globe. His only rival for the title of greatest operatic tenor in the world is Placido Domingo.**

**I've been sleeping** completely naked with the window wide open – even in winter – ever since I saw a film in which Anthony Quinn lived happily in an igloo. My wife, who feels the cold, didn't like the idea of wearing nothing in bed, but when she noticed how warm I was, she was convinced that it was a good idea. I used to wrap up night and day, and I even went to bed with a scarf on. Yet I caught more colds than ever before. When I'm on tour I make sure I get 12 hours' rest before a performance. I wear earplugs. When I wake I practise exercises at full volume for half an hour, which must be heard by many hotel guests. Still, it's never before 9 o'clock.

I never have breakfast. I go for a short walk when I'm on tour and relax in the morning. For lunch before a performance I have roast beef or steak, both underdone. And a little wine. Then I sleep for 20 minutes to digest peacefully. Generally, I don't talk before a performance, but today is an exception. I arrive an hour and a half before a performance and test my voice for five minutes – scales, arpeggios, a few exercises – then I do my own make-up. My beard hides weaknesses around the chin.

Of course I'm not supposed to eat sugar or fat, but today I'm having a biscuit because I have a performance. Any weight I put on won't stay for long because I lose 4lb during a performance – a combination of energy expended, the heat in the opera house, perspiring inside heavy costumes, and, of course, nerves.

I eat after a performance, never before. A salad without meat refreshes me, and if I can't get my local wine – Lambrusco, which sparkles and is drunk cold – I add ice and soda to Valpolicella or Chianti and imagine I'm at home in Italy. The great Ferraris and Maseratis are made in my home town of Modena. They're fast and beautiful. But I drive a Mercedes. Not an automatic – have you ever seen an Italian without a gear stick? I need a stick for I'm surrounded at home by women: my wife, three daughters, my sister, my wife's sister and two dogs. In Modena I visit the espresso bars and chat to friends I used to play football with – I was in Modena's soccer team till I took up singing

I am faithful to my wife. Why not? I said this once on TV. I suppose no one believed me, but it is true

# LADY DIANA COOPER
## AUGUST 13, 1978

**Lady Diana Cooper, Viscountess Norwich, was born in 1892. Famed for her classic beauty, she married the late writer-politician Duff Cooper in 1919. She lives alone in Little Venice, London.**

**I'm a bad** sleeper now and wake early, around 7. It's not like those days when one got in from a ball, counted eight hours on the fingers and said: "Call me for lunch." I make myself a tankard of lovely hot chocolate. That's my breakfast. Extraordinary when I look back at the breakfasts we used to have: all those silver dishes on the sideboard looking like gigantic boiled eggs and filled with kedgeree, kidneys and chicken legs. No wonder we were all fat, even the ballerinas.

Normally I'll stay in bed until lunchtime. It's warm, and my telephone and reference books are within reach. Getting up takes time. I also wear a lot of make-up – it *is* more difficult growing old if one has been thought beautiful. No facelifts, but I am painted an inch thick. I don't think I'm vain. I never admired myself much. Don't like my type. I fasted for 21 days once and used to laugh when Gandhi was making a fuss about doing it for 48 hours. I used to entertain a lot but now a luncheon party is a rare treat. My son's Filipino comes over and does everything. Harold Macmillan always enjoys himself. He keeps the table in a roar till after 4 o'clock. He does like to sparkle. I can't think why

## I don't think I'm vain. I never admired myself much. Don't like my type

he lives such a stupid life in the country. When the Queen Mother comes to lunch I have to make sure she goes to the right loo. I've hung all my royalty photographs in the one downstairs. She might feel rather insulted.

I do go out in the evening but I can't bear balls because the noise is so appalling. I'm perfectly happy with the telly. I've got it in the bedroom, of course, with one of those remote-control things. I get the greatest pleasure watching cheetahs and things and Bamber Gascoigne with University Challenge. I have one or two friends who know that I don't sleep, so they telephone around 1 or 2 in the morning. Of course a lot of friends are dying. I get used to that. They're doing it all the time, and those who aren't are losing their marbles. It's really my profession now, visiting the marbleless.

**Lady Diana Cooper died in 1986, at 93. She is survived by her son, John Julius Norwich, the 2nd Viscount Norwich.**

at 19. My daughters are lovely. I miss my wife when I'm away, but a mother is needed at home. I am away 40 days at a stretch, then stay home 15 days. I am faithful to my wife. Why not? I said this once on a live TV programme in New York. I suppose no one believed me, but it is true.

And now I must shut my mouth or I shall not be able to sing well tonight at Covent Garden. I shall sleep for 20 minutes, then I will gargle with Listerine before leaving for the Opera House. **Luciano Pavarotti was divorced from his wife in 2000, after 35 years of marriage. His new partner, Nicoletta Mantovani, 33, gave birth to their daughter, Alice, in January 2003.**

I can't give you the exact acreage of my loo, but a family of 12 could live in it. In fact are living in it

**PETER COOK, COMIC ACTOR**

80s

# PETER COOK
## AUGUST 5, 1984

**Peter Cook, anarchic wit and comic actor, lives in Hampstead, London, and 'in the country' with his wife, the actress Judy Huxtable. He has two teenage daughters from his first marriage.**

**I breakfast in** the bathroom, where I have a very nice statue of Dorothy Squires. She has always been my inspiration. I collect my thoughts while being shaved by my Personal Daintiness people. I can't give you the exact acreage of my loo – I don't want to make your readers envious – but a family of 12 could live in it. In fact *are* living in it. They are mainly dissidents (who have been complaining lately about being out of fashion. They come over here expecting to be greeted with champagne and jobs at the BBC, and now they're living in my bathroom...). My beauty routine is a mixture of aerobics, isotonics, isometrics and a little yoga. To the observer it would look as if I was merely lifting a cup of coffee to my lips and lighting a cigarette. But through mental control you are in fact exercising every muscle in your body and clearing the brain of all the toxins that gather while asleep.

Quite a lot of famous people tend to drop by, like Jonathan Miller; but if no one does, I might rummage through a large cardboard box – always something to do in solitude. I hardly ever seem to leave Hampstead these days. When I do, weird things seem to happen to me. Recently a taxi driver pointed out a factory which he said makes the best artificial limbs in the world. Douglas Bader got his from there. "Of course, there are advantages to being limbless," he said. "Put it this way. Sir Douglas Bader would not have been famous if he had had legs." I get a lot of remarks like this from total strangers. John Cleese swears I attract them somehow.

In the evening, I might go dancing, which I love. But I hate the theatre because you can't smoke and I like to keep up to my target of 40 a day. I never get to sleep before 2 or 3 in the morning, due to the way my metabolism works. If I really want to go to sleep I read one of Clive James's long, boring poems. That's not anti-Clive. They're really very relaxing.
**Peter Cook died in 1995 at 57 from a gastrointestinal haemorrhage.**

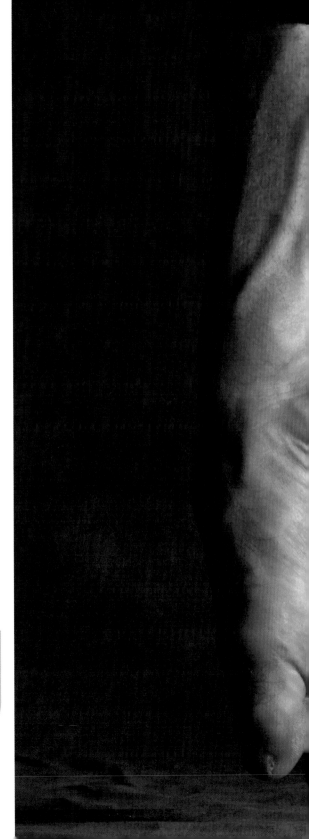

# RUDOLF NUREYEV

## MAY 5, 1985

**The ballet dancer Rudolf Nureyev, 46, was born to poor Tartar parents aboard a train to Vladivostok, and leapt to freedom in 1961. He is now director of the Ballet de l'Opéra in Paris, where he was photographed by Lord Snowdon.**

**Morning is the** most difficult time for me. I often don't want to get up, but I have found a remedy that always works. It's simply a question of whether I have a bath first, and tea after, or tea first, and a bath after. I put on something casual, like velvet trousers and a shirt or jumper, then have breakfast about 9 o'clock. No, I don't prepare it myself. Thank God, I can at least afford to have someone to cook, do my laundry and clean my apartment. I have a maid who brings me two pieces of hot, buttered toast, marmalade and lots of tea. Tea is my weakness. I take it without milk and keep a flask with me, so I can drink it all day long.

My overriding priority each day is to be in good physical form. I go to class from 10 to 12 noon to build up my mental and physical strength. I perform about 40 times a season with the company, but I still dance separately 20 to 30 times a year. I get nervous before every performance. Often the mind is ready, but the body

## I give everything, stretch myself to the utmost. It is simply a question of will

isn't – it doesn't follow the patterns you want it to. Once on stage I give everything. Each time I stretch myself to the utmost. It is simply a question of will. You learn to switch yourself on and off. I stopped expecting perfection a long time ago, but I always demand the maximum from myself and those I work with.

Some evenings I go out with dancers from the company for dinner, and we combine talking shop with relaxing. I don't have any food fads, but I'm very fond of vodka. I don't smoke, don't go to nightclubs. and only occasionally go to parties. My favourite form of socialising is to have friends round to my apartment. For the first time in a long while I feel I've got a home, apart from my dressing room! I've bought an apartment overlooking the Seine and furnished it in a very romantic style. I had the interior designed by an Italian but I insisted on my set of Russian birchwood chairs. I find it all very comfortable and in excellent taste. But when a friend came to see it, his first comment was, "Ah, still Cossack!" Such prejudice!

**Rudolf Nureyev died in Paris in January 1993 of cardiac complications resulting from Aids. He was 54.**

# ANDY WARHOL

APRIL 20, 1980

**Andy Warhol, 53, is an icon of pop art, famous for his paintings of Campbell's soup cans. His films, Sleep (a six-hour film of a man sleeping) and The Chelsea Girls, packed cinemas in the 1960s. Since then he has been by turns adored, vilified and, in 1969, shot at. He now edits his own magazine, Interview.**

**My secretary calls** me around 8.30 and we discuss what I did the night before. I don't eat anything or drink anything, not even orange juice, because I've usually had at least three dinners the night before. I wear the same clothes every day – jeans, a striped shirt with a white collar and tie. I have a marvellous girl who fixes it so that whenever I open the closet door there is a clean set of clothes ready.

The office is 49 blocks from my house and I walk halfway before I pick up a cab. I'll spend the morning seeing people who call at the office with portfolios of their work. We have this magazine called Interview and we're always trying to find new talent. One complication is that I have usually gone round New York the night before offering the front cover to everybody I meet. So Bob [Bob Colacello, his chief executive] has to untangle all that. Poor Bob's had a bad press recently. The British newspapers called him The Shark. I like that, but he was very hurt, so I make jokes about it to take away the pain. Sweet, huh? Bob's been with me for nine years now and he makes everything work. On my own, just me, I couldn't get into or out of a hotel. I sign the cheque. I tend to worry more about providing one free copy of the new book we're promoting for a nice waiter rather than worry about a hundred copies for people that I've never met.

In the afternoon I try to paint. I have this room behind the elevator. I don't let anyone in. I don't always succeed in painting, but I keep on trying. I don't actually like my paintings very much. I don't hang them in my house. I'd rather go out and buy very simple American primitives. They're really nice to live with.

I go home around 7. I feel slightly bad about that. The rest of the kids work 9 through 6, but it suits me to start later and stay later, so somebody has to stay with me. If there are any other kids still around when I leave, I'll drop them off in my cab. I need to go home to change my shirt and have dinner with my dogs – Amos and Archie; they are dachshunds. I *love* my dogs. They eat what I eat. I don't do anything fancy like lay the table, it's just eat and run. If you want to know about a really good evening in my life, you should ask Bob for specific details. Everything kind of merges for me. I usually start off at a dinner party. I never ask anybody on a date. It's so hard to do that – I'd spend all day thinking about how I was going to organise it.

Because of our magazine I get invited to a lot of promos [promotions]. There's always a party for a new book, or a club opening, or a fashion show. I really do like fashion – not for me to wear, because it would take up too

## I don't actually like my paintings very much. I don't hang them in my house

much of my time, but to look at on other people. I'm kind of keen about saving time up. I like furniture, really good furniture, but you have to spend time looking after it, so I end up filling my house with things that nobody else wants, 1920s stuff, or, best of all, hotel furniture – pretty and not at all comfortable.

It's kind of funny what makes people comfortable. I like movies, but I can't enjoy anything in a crowded cinema so I go to screenings in small private movie theatres. I can't stand any of my old movies. None.

It's a neat life. There's nobody I ever want to be with particularly. My friends are everybody who's there in front of me. If I ever have problems I shall discuss them with Bianca Jagger, who is not only beautiful and intelligent and talented and a great actress and dancer but also very sensible. Or I might go to my doctor. But I've never been to a psychiatrist. People in New York don't believe in the efficacy of psychiatry any more. They're going back to church. I've never been away – I go to the small Roman Catholic church round the corner from my house most Sundays. But I haven't been to confession for some while. I have nothing to confess. **Andy Warhol died of a heart attack in 1987 in New York after an operation on his gall-bladder.**

# CARY GRANT

## FEBRUARY 1, 1981

**Cary Grant, born in Bristol in 1904, made 70 films between 1932 and 1966. Since then he has concentrated on his business interests. He lives with his fifth wife, Barbara, in Beverly Hills.**

I never was interested in the storylines of my movies. Just the business interest

**I suffer from** insomnia. Always have. I usually wake around three and read for an hour or so. Never fiction. If it's not true, what's the point of it? I never was interested in the storylines of my movies. Just the business interest. Do you know I'm still getting a nice return on To Catch a Thief? Marvellous deal there. My houseman leaves a tray outside our bedroom door with an orange, not peeled or de-pipped but sliced into four equal parts. I teeth off the flesh from the skin. Marvellous.

I've never understood why people are so surprised at an actor taking to business. If an actor can get three million bucks for 10 weeks' work, he's no dope where business is concerned. Picasso was the greatest businessman I ever knew. Eight dollars' worth of paint and a bit of canvas, and if he said he'd let you have it for $350,000, you said: "Hold it right there while I run round to the bank."

Most mornings I deal with my solicitors. In the afternoon – oh, Barbara, what *do* I do in the afternoon? Just more of the same, I guess. Certainly I don't crook a finger to keep fit. Barbara thinks I'm fit now because I started life as an acrobat. When I was 12 I dearly wanted to travel. I worked out that circus people get to travel, so I ran off and tried to join. It happened that the leader of the circus was a Mason and so was my father. They came to an arrangement and when I was 14 I left home to travel the world as an acrobat.

We like a very quiet life. We have a wonderful couple who look after us, the houseman and his wife. Both marvellous cooks, so we have meals at home. We watch television sometimes. More often we play cards. Do you know Spite and Malice? Marvellous game. We have a few close friends. We see a lot of the Gregory Pecks. More of them than anybody else.

We go to bed sometimes at 8 o'clock, sometimes at 12. In my view there's nothing worth doing once it's got dark. Who needs nightclubs? They're just full of sick people smoking, drinking. I can't stand cigarette smoke. Won't have anybody near me who smokes. I'm not extravagant. I'm still wearing the same shoes I wore in the

# JANET CRESSWELL
## MARCH 15, 1987

Janet Cresswell, 55, was sent to Broadmoor 10 years ago for wounding a psychiatrist in protest at the authorities' refusal to investigate the cause of her psychiatric problems. She has one daughter.

**The doors open** and the lights go on at 7am. I could never understand the point of getting up at all if there was nothing useful to do, but those at Broadmoor feel differently. After breakfast at 8, my friend and I play Scrabble: it helps pass boredom time while medication is dispensed. It puzzles me that there is so little outcry against psychiatric medicines – I have needed three gynae operations to counteract the drugs I was forced to have some years ago.

When "All work areas and school" is called over the Tannoy, we assemble until our escorts are ready and the nurse on radio control has signalled we can move. Chaos reigns until we are at work. I am in the sewing room, but not because I can sew. I am employed replacing buttons on kitchen overalls or turning up nurses' uniforms. Before I came to Broadmoor, for stabbing a psychiatrist in the backside, I regarded myself as useless at handiwork. After 10 years I still feel I am useless but now accept that Broadmoor does not want me to do anything I am good at.

Once a fortnight, we women are driven to revolution point when volunteer men come over for a chat. This is called a

## I now accept Broadmoor does not want me to do anything I am good at

"games evening", and the women have to attend. This is one of the few forced social events and a case for women's liberation. Mugshots are renewed each time we change hairstyle, or every five years. One recent escapee, a friend whom I miss enormously, hopped off from an outing when reaching the underwear section of Marks & Spencer. She has a gentle face and her photo on television gave the reverse impression of the description given of her. Looking far more manic, the MP who appeared on BBC raved that killers should not be allowed on outings from Broadmoor. I quite agree, but realise the definition of who is a danger to the public is somewhat exaggerated.

I am rarely sad to get locked up again at 9pm. I don't have night sedation. I have a clear conscience: the only things that keep me awake are the flashing of the nurses' torches and their heavy footsteps as they come round on their night inspection. **Janet Cresswell remains in Broadmoor to this day.**

days when I was making those old movies of mine. Always had them made in London. But this jacket I got in Hong Kong. And Jaeger's – you know, that's a wonderful business – very kindly made me this cable-stitched sweater specially. They'd dropped them from stock and they knew how much I like them.

I'm not too hassled about clothes. Should I be at my age? I don't feel my age. Not often, anyway. But I don't have a magic formula. I used to have a vodka before dinner, but I've given that up now. If I have a secret at all it's that I do just what I want. I think that stops the ageing process as much as anything.
**Cary Grant died in 1986, aged 82.**

# CHRISTIAN LACROIX
## AUGUST 27, 1989

**The French fashion designer Christian Lacroix, 38, made headlines with his design for the puffball skirt in 1987. He works closely with his live-in muse and companion, Françoise Rosensthiel, in Paris.**

**I wake up** like clockwork at 7.30am. For an important lunch I prefer a well-made Italian three-piece suit and I like to mix styles: a striped shirt, a Paisley pocket handkerchief and a spotted tie... Fashion writers call me dandy. Some designers lead lives as luxurious as their clients', but that's not my style. I look upon a couturier as a tradesman, as he was in the past. A favourite client is Paloma Picasso. Like me, she loves bulls. Bulls are in my blood. My parents took me to a bullfight when I was three and I am still fascinated by blood in the arena, though I will cry if I see a cat run over. I hate the sight of my own blood, which I see quite often as I have blood tests and cardiographs taken regularly because I tire quickly. It is tough being in the limelight. I was overwhelmed by the publicity that followed my first collection. But I am wary of the press. I may be on top today, but I could fall from favour at a stroke. I don't ever want to be a prisoner of an image, so I shall keep my feet on the ground.

Françoise is my muse. I couldn't work without her. I think of her, talk of her, laugh with her. I remember my first glimpse of this perfect example of the true Parisienne. It was as if I had been struck by lightning. She is pretty and full of wit. I am taciturn and incapable of making others laugh. We talk about having children, but

## I don't ever want to be a prisoner of an image. I shall keep my feet on the ground

we're pessimistic about the future. There's Le Pen and the National Front, the Mediterranean is so polluted...

Nowadays I tend to come home after dinner and work with the television on. There was a time when I went to nightclubs, although I soon got bored with nightlife in Paris. But in the south there are festivals and there I really can be happy and dance on the table almost all night.

**Lacroix married his muse, Françoise, in 1991. He is still based in Paris, and now has exclusive stores in New York, London, Geneva and Japan. He also works in theatre design.**

# DANIEL HARVEY

## JUNE 23, 1985

**Daniel Harvey, 9, attends Gosforth Park First School, Newcastle-upon-Tyne, where he plays midfield for the seven-a-side team. He lives with his parents and brother, James, 7. He wrote to tell us about his day.**

**I get up** at 7.30. Well, I actually get up at 7.34 because I like a bit of a lie-in. I get dressed and do a bit of colouring and then comes the call that always comes: "Daniel, breakfast's ready!" That's my mum. I go downstairs and find my Beano has come. "Hi, Mum" is my usual phrase. I sit down and pour out the Coco Pops. "Do you know where the free plastic animal is?" I say. "I don't know," Mum says. "James might have got it." James, my brother, is a pain, I think to myself. Here he is now – speak of the devil.

After breakfast Mum says: "Get your football kit, it's Thursday, remember." Ding-dong, the doorbell rings. "That'll be Paul," I say. I go to answer the door. "Hello, Paul," I say. "We'll be there in a minute." Paul is my school friend. Soon we are walking down the road. I think I've seen Stevie. I'll swing my bag around my head and if he swings his around his head I'll know it's him. I run to meet him. The rest of the way to school we keep a sharp look out for the big 'uns, especially the boy with the green jacket. "Wally" is our name for him.

My teacher, Mr Gibson, calls the register: Michael, Jason, and so on until we get to Emma. "I've forgotten my dinner money," she says. "That's the fourth time this week," says Mr Gibson. The first part of the morning goes the way most mornings go, then it's playtime at 10.30. We go outside, shouting and talking, and play tuggie-round-the-shed just outside the school. Anthony falls over. Oh dear, I forgot to mention the TV programme we watch at 10 o'clock called How We Used to Live. It's about how we used to live, obviously. Well, back to the present. We are told to do maths until lunchtime. I like maths.

It's lunch now – fish and chips and peas. I don't like peas. It's semolina for pudding. I don't like it. Now it's squad. We get changed and soon we're outside and trying to get our boots on. Stevie, our school team captain, takes the balls out onto the football field. We normally have a bit of a kick around until Mr Gibson comes out. He picks captains and then he picks players. I'm normally a centre forward. I do all the goal scoring. Well, I do a bit of the goal scoring. But I hardly ever score any goals. I don't know why, but I just keep missing the goal by about a foot.

We finish squad at about 1pm and come in and get changed. We sit on the carpet and Mr Gibson comes in and sits down in his chair and says, "Right, we're going to do language," and I groan because I don't like language. It's boring. He tells us to do Section 11, Book 3 and we go and sit down with our books, which we fight over for about 15 minutes. Mr Gibson always says: "Fifteen minutes ago I was talking about language – why are there 43 people wandering about?" There are mutters about how there

## I hardly ever score. I don't know why, but I just keep on missing the goal

aren't 30 people in the class, never mind 43. Finally we get settled down and work, and anybody who doesn't won't go out for games. At 2.19 Claire, our school bellringer, gets up and goes to ring the bell, *ringg, ringgg, ringgg*.

At play we play fight-busters, a group of people set up by me and Malcolm that stops the third years fighting, but doesn't stop *us* fighting very much. After play it's games and you normally hear *cluck cluck* as we try to get our boots on. Boots can be hard to get on.

The way back from school is much the same as the way there, so I don't have to talk about that. While Lucy, our babysitter, gets my tea I watch all the programmes for children. My favourite is called Monkey. It's about some Chinese warriors and their adventures. At half past six Mr Gibson comes round and takes us to a stamp club where somebody comes and talks about stamps he or she has put together. This finishes at 9 and I help to put the stands away. Mr Gibson has a medal because this year he is president of the stamp club. Then I go home and go to bed after a hard day.

**Daniel, now 28, is a medical senior house officer in cardiology at a Nottingham hospital. He plans to train in anaesthesia and hopes eventually to become a specialist in critical-care medicine. His girlfriend is also a doctor.**

34

# PRINCESS MICHAEL OF KENT

## APRIL 29, 1984

**HRH Princess Michael of Kent, born in Carlsbad, Bohemia, married Prince Michael in 1978. They live in Kensington Palace and in Gloucestershire with their children, Frederick, 5, and Gabriella, 3. Princess Michael wrote her own Life in the Day.**

**It is my** husband's military training that gets me up early. He makes me ride in all weathers; that is why I usually have a cold. My breakfast consists of china tea and bran, which I hate, on a tray. I try to dress and make up and take telephone calls and play with Freddie and Ella all at the same time. Usually the children and the cats eat the bran and I get make-up all over the phone. Mornings I spend at my desk in my office in the basement, with Julia, who is a treasure and looks after my clothes. I try to fit in one or two tennis sessions a week at Queen's Club. I play with a pro. It's the way I work out my frustrations. My husband calls me a cupboard cat because I really like to spend life curled up somewhere warm and snug.

Lunch is something not fattening, cold ham or chicken, if my husband is at home. If I am alone I often join Ella in the nursery as Freddie now goes to proper school. As a European I find four years old very young to go to real school with a uniform; as for boarding school at eight, my heart sinks, but I know they love it and I must give in. I rarely go shopping – the office does most of it by telephone. The little bit I do shop I do abroad, because I have more time and I am less conspicuous. Lots of the children's clothes come from Marks & Spencer.

I rarely spend long stretches of time with the children but see them often for short times. I am impatient and I do not want them to see me cross. My husband has great patience and spends hours with Freddie doing Lego, with the little girl on his knee. Between 5 and 6 I go up to the nursery for tea with them. They both talk a lot and the cats join in, hoping for bits to fall from the table: rather medieval in a way. After tea there are a few games and a bath. I try to stay out of trouble but sometimes they persuade me to wash them and I get rather wet. I have to tell a Griselda story. She is a witch I invented, with a motorbike engine on her broomstick. She eats little fat children. But it saddens me that they sing German nursery rhymes with an English accent, as their father is a great linguist – he speaks Russian fluently. At 6 it is time

My husband calls me a cupboard cat, because I like to spend life curled up somewhere warm and snug

# MICHAEL CAINE
## MAY 27, 1984

**Michael Caine, born in Rotherhithe, southeast London, in 1933, became a major movie star with Alfie in 1966. He now lives in Beverly Hills with his wife, Shakira, and their daughter, Natasha, 10.**

**I've totally accepted** the American way of life. We have a very high standard of living, but not in a stupid way. We don't have mink-lined, kidney-shaped swimming pools. I could retire now, but like most people from poor backgrounds I have an insecurity about money. I'd have to have three times what I needed before I'd think of it. I do miss England a bit. I still love London, no matter what they do with it.

But I can be out of the pool and down to Beverly Hills for a business meeting in minutes. It's having the best of both worlds. I love it. Sitting out there by the pool is like being in the south of France. Except that you can understand the television. When I'm not working – because when I'm filming I wouldn't be here anyway – I usually rise late, say around 9.30, sunbathe, swim, snooze, play tennis, have a sauna, go out to a party, go to bed. Typically exhausting day. I have a glass of fresh grapefruit juice – I don't know anyone here who bothers with breakfast. I do it in England, all that heart attack on a plate. Sausage, bacon, eggs, tomatoes, white bread and butter, and tea with milk and sugar. The heart-attack rate in England is still rising because of

# Sunbathe, swim, snooze, go to a party, go to bed. Typically exhausting day

that bloody breakfast. But I do miss Melton Mowbray pies. We've got four cars – a Rolls-Royce Silver Wraith II, then there's an old American banger, a Volkswagen station wagon and the new VW saloon. When you go to a party here there are two questions you don't ask: "How's the wife?" and "Are you working?" You wait for them to tell you – if they want to. Things can happen very quickly in this town, and you never know who might be with whom. I see people like Rod Stewart, Barbra Streisand, Dudley Moore...

At the moment I'm dickering over a film that would take five months in Tunisia. But Shakira and I have never been separated for more than four weeks before, and our little one is at school here. So unless they make me an offer I can't refuse...
**Michael Caine won his second Oscar in 2000, in which year he was also knighted – under his real name, Maurice Micklewhite – and made a Bafta fellow.**

for a much-needed drink. It is also time to get ready for the evening's official engagement if there is one, read the file, choose the clothes. If we do not go out I cook and we read or watch TV. Now we watch our figures, so it is usually simple. Sadly my husband does not play bridge. I miss that. We entertain little and like being on our own. Our private pleasures are really a night at the opera or theatre and travel. We long to do another journey as we did in India, which was wonderful; and on our honeymoon in Iran – we were the Shah's last visitors. I always read before sleep. My ambition is to write a good book, then to get a history degree – and to make the cover of Horse & Hound on merit.

# BIG DADDY

## FEBRUARY 22, 1981

**Shirley Crabtree, 47, known to wrestling fans as Big Daddy, lives in his native Yorkshire with his second wife, Eunice, and daughter, Jane, 11. His father, also a wrestler, gave him his first lesson.**

**I'm usually wrestling** six nights a week and I don't get home till the small hours. So I get up quite late – about 10. I meditate for about 20 minutes, saying prayers, preparing for the day ahead. Then I go off to the moors with my bull terrier, Patch. He's full of energy, leaping over 6ft walls – I can't tire him out. I carry a hundredweight sack for stamina training. And I love the solitude. When I get back I have a light breakfast. If I'm at home I answer the fan mail, which my wife, Eunice, has sorted out. I get hundreds of letters a week, mostly from children or people in hospital.

Lunch is my one big meal. I have to be careful. I don't want to regret what I've eaten when I'm pounding and bumping in the ring that night. Most afternoons I visit someone who has written to me from a hospital near the venue. I like just to pop in. As soon as Big Daddy walks into a ward, everyone starts laughing. They like it if I wear one of my ring outfits – spangly top hats, multicoloured cloaks and sequined leotards. Eunice designs them for me. The attraction of wrestling is very basic. It's the fascination of seeing two men stripped off in some kind of combat. And there's a touch of the old music hall. The audiences can cheer, hiss, shout – it's entertainment for the whole family. And as to charges that it's fixed, how

## I step out and I know this is what I'm meant to do, just like an old circus horse

could you rehearse a different match every night?

Before I go on, I can feel the adrenaline starting. Then I step out and with the first smiling face I see, I know this is what I'm meant to do – just like an old circus horse. I come on, to my signature tune, We Shall Not Be Moved. The other night I had Scots Guards in bearskins with pipers to accompany me – I used to be a guardsman myself. I don't win all my matches, but I'm philosophical. Losing is part of living, and you've got to accept it. If you can lose with dignity it can be magnificent.

**Big Daddy died after suffering a stroke in 1997.**

# CYNTHIA PAYNE

## SEPTEMBER 9, 1984

**Cynthia Payne, aka Madam Cyn, won notoriety with her sex parties for middle-aged and elderly men in Streatham, London. She spent four months in Holloway Prison for keeping a disorderly house.**

**Since the raid** my life's been humdrum. When my father died I inherited a few thousand, but his money's going now. I have thought about opening a brothel in Belgium, where it's legal. Before I got raided my life was so different. I've had so much happen these last four years – people dying: my father, the squadron leader ["Mitch", an old friend]... I would love to get started again. But I'm not a real madam. Mitch used to call me Mme Baloney, and that's true. But the tax people didn't believe it: they thought I had thousands of pounds abroad or something.

People think I gave the parties for a kinky thrill. But for me there's nothing sexual in it. It can be very boring to me – after two abortions, I'm not particularly interested in sex. It's just that it makes people happy. Sex doesn't embarrass me, never has done. It's like having a cup of tea. I do have a lot of men come and tell me about their sexual deviations. I don't laugh at them. I'm terribly fascinated to know *why* people want a beating, why they like a particular kink. I want to go into their childhood. You have to be a bit of a psychologist to run a brothel.

People trust me more now, which is a heavy burden to bear. They come up to me and say, "I've just done six months in prison," and I'm shocked, because I'm a prude. I think going to prison for stealing is terrible. They think because I've gone to prison I'll understand. But I don't. I know it looks as if I should be bitter towards men in general but I've got a good living out of prostitution – a lovely house. My life was comparatively easy running a brothel. Agreed, I had a lot of raids, but in any job you've got aggravation. Now it's a completely new life and it's not easy. I meet new friends, but they're not tested friends.

There were eight women in my room in Holloway. I was the only sex case. It took a month for them to accept me, because they had preconceived ideas of what a madam was like. It's very explosive in there. Their lives are so boring that if they can find fault with you, they will. The screws used to shove all the lesbians in my room. We got on very well. I was the old lady – it was always "Mrs Payne". They were much kinder to their own sex than

## You have to be a bit of a psychologist to run a brothel. I'm fascinated to know just why people like a beating

## PADDINGTON BEAR

### SEPTEMBER 8, 1985

**Paddington Bear, Peru's most famous expatriate, was christened in 1958 after the station near which his 'minder', Michael Bond, then lived. He describes his day, with help from Mr Bond.**

**I have an** alarm clock set for 7.30 each morning. As soon as it stops ringing I get out of bed and draw the curtains. If it's raining I'll put on my wellington boots and get back into bed for an extra five minutes. Sometimes, if there isn't an R in the month, I take a bath. Otherwise I have what Mrs Bird calls "a lick and a promise". Bears' fur goes soggy very easily, so I have to be careful. For breakfast, I have a boiled egg followed by toast and marmalade. Mrs Bird takes the top off the egg because it's a bit messy with paws. I like home-made marmalade with chunks that are big enough to be used for other things. If there are any left over after breakfast I wrap them up and put them under my hat in case I have emergency repairs to make during the day.

After breakfast I collect the morning shopping list from Mrs Bird. Then I get my basket on wheels out from under the stairs and set off for the Portobello Road. Bears are good at shopping. They drive a hard bargain. I'm well known in the market and most of the traders let me squeeze the fruit and vegetables before buying, just like they do in Peru. They can still say it's untouched by hand. Being a bear has lots of advantages.

## If it's raining, I'll put on my wellington boots and get back into bed

Every day I call in at the baker's, where I have a standing order for buns. Then I visit my friend, Mr Gruber. Mr Gruber keeps an antique shop in the Portobello Road and always has some hot cocoa ready for our elevenses. When I get back home I have a snack and then I go upstairs to answer my mail. Often there are 50 fan letters a week, mostly from America. If I have time, I send a postcard to my Aunt Lucy, who is in the home for Retired Bears in Lima.

In the evening I have dinner with the Brown family. My favourite is stew with dumplings and jam. I went to France once and ate something called "novel cuisine". It didn't seem very novel to me. After that I go upstairs and wind my alarm clock for the next day. I sleep very soundly and I never snore. I stayed awake one night to find out and I didn't do it even once.

**More than 30m copies of 70 Paddington Bear books have now been sold in 30 different languages around the world.**

the ordinary women. I think the screws were sorry to see me go, because I kept morale high. At 4pm, when we were locked up for the day, I'd always say to the girls: "Another day gone." And if a girl was crying I'd say: "Just keep telling yourself this isn't going to last for ever." That's how I calmed them down, and myself too.

I don't regret anything I've done, even when I went to prison. I said to myself: "Well, it was worth it for the life I've had for about the last 15 years." Because I never really wanted to lead a humdrum life.

**Cynthia Payne had a one-woman show at the Edinburgh Fringe Festival in 1992 and is making a living as an after-dinner speaker.**

# JEFFREY ARCHER

## JUNE 8, 1986

**Jeffrey Archer, 46, a bright young hope of the Tories, resigned in 1974 in order to rebuild his fortune after an unwise investment. His novel Not a Penny More, Not a Penny Less was the first of five bestsellers. Now Conservative party deputy chairman, he, his wife, Mary, and two sons live in London and Grantchester.**

**I'm a 6** o'clock waker – very much a lark, not an owl. Then I like to spend 30 minutes just thinking – planning the day. I do think busy people have a tendency to do no thinking. It's all action, action, action. Clothes and so on are all things that have to be got out of the way. I shop once every two years on a Friday afternoon and get a dozen pairs of socks and a dozen pairs of pants and a dozen shorts – made by an Irishman called Mr Fisherty, behind Jaeger.

If I'm at home writing I take my younger son to school. The older one used to complain when I took him, because I was the only father: "The other boys think you're out of work." But the writer does have that privilege. I like to be at my desk at 9.30 when I'm writing a book, but I only work two hours on the trot. From 9.30 to 11.30. Around 1,000 words. I never know what's on the next line, the next page, how it will end. I honestly believe that if I knew, you'd know. When I wrote First Among Equals, I didn't know who was going to be the prime minister until I reached the last page.

I can't type. I handwrite every word and my secretary puts it on the word processor. Then I write over it. I do six drafts of every book. The early ones drove her mad. Afterwards I go for a walk – to think through what I've written. Ten times around the garden, then I go back. I'm totally self-disciplined. I've sold 25m copies of my books, but I'm very cautious with money now, after the downfall.

I usually have lunch in a local pub. I'm very traditional and I love nanny's food – shepherd's pie, lancashire hotpot. I inevitably end up watching 30 to 45 minutes of television, especially if there's an old Jack Hawkins film, or some cricket. That relaxes me for the afternoon session. Between 3 and 5, I go over the morning's work. Then I'll pick up James from school and go and watch his rugger or cricket or athletics.

I hate holidays. But I have one every four years which I adore, and it's called the Olympic Games. And now I've taken a complete break from writing until the next election. It's out of the question to write at the same time. This life is very different. I still get up early and take a car over to Central Office, where I have two secretaries.

I have access to what the chairman, Norman Tebbit, is doing, but my main job is going out into the constituencies. Ministers are so overloaded that no one goes to see the troops, but my aim is to go to 300 before the election. I have zero interest in getting back into parliament. I loved it between the ages of 29 and 34. I'm now 46 and it hasn't the same appeal to have a constituency with 50,000 demanding people.

I get most pleasure from my lunches, where I invite 10

# I do think busy people have a tendency to do no thinking. It's all action, action, action

people together who wouldn't normally meet. They are always men and I must have met them or worked with them, because you must be able to tease them. I once put Harrison Ford and Leon Brittan next to each other. Later I heard Leon trying to explain who was next to him: "A tall, good-looking American." They got on terribly well.

I read a lot at weekends. My favourite book is Robert Blake's Disraeli. Disraeli is so fascinating because he's both a great politician and a great writer and the combination is devastating. The manager at Hatchards quite often says: "You must read this..." I get 10 books a year from him. I've always believed you should trust professionals.

**Four months later, Archer wrote the second resignation letter of his career, amid allegations of involvement with a prostitute, Monica Coghlan. In 1987 he won £500,000 damages from The Star and £50,000 from the News of the World. Archer was made a life peer in 1992. Seven years later he quit as Tory candidate for London mayor after being accused of fabricating an alibi in his 1987 libel case. In July 2001 he was found guilty of perverting the course of justice and perjury. He received a four-year sentence and was sent to Belmarsh Prison as prisoner number FF8282.**

# STANLEY GREEN

## APRIL 14, 1985

**Stanley Green, 70, is Oxford Street's most famous 'sandwichman', promoting his theory that 'less protein means less lust'. In his bedsit near Harrow he hand-prints the booklets he sells at 11p a copy.**

**Every other day** bread has to be made that will rise when I'm at work and I'll bake it when I come home. I have porridge for breakfast, and then I'll finish off the booklets I've printed and stapled the previous night. By then it's 8am and the dinner has to be prepared. That is done on the Bunsen burner. I wash while it's cooking. One can exist completely as a vegetarian if one knows what one is up to. I don't need passion, you see. I live on steamed vegetables, lentils or pulses. And a pound of apples a day.

I now have a free travel pass. I used to cycle into London. Jolly hard work, too. With the wind against me it could take two hours. I fixed up a frame on the rear of the bicycle and my board could be read by motorists. People would toot and wave. I've known coaches pass and everyone has stood up and cheered. I come out of the Underground at Oxford Circus, then assemble my board on the least windy corner. In the war, when I was 30, I was astonished when things were said quite openly – what a husband would say to his wife when home on leave. I've always been a moral sort of person. When I decided to go on the street, I knew protein made passion from my own experience. Protein wisdom changes your whole life, makes it easier. Passion can be a great torment.

I have my dinner at about 2.30, in a warm and secret place. I'm not doing any harm – I am doing a public service. Half-past four, that's when the peak starts, and then it's quite a sensation. I give people all I've got as they are hurrying by. I've been in a police court twice. The injustice of it upsets me because I'm doing such a good job. I'm on the street till 6.30, then I come home. I arrive back some nights and there's spittle in the middle of my hat. Once some youths put phlegm on their palms, patted me on the back and rubbed it in. That's why I wear a green overall. I do understand human nature. If you're not willing to forgive people, you become very cynical.

I try and put my head on the pillow at about 12.30. I do, from habit, say my own prayer. Quite a good prayer, unselfish too. It is a sort of acknowledgment of God, just in case there happens to be one.

**Stanley Green died in 1993. His sandwichboard and three boxes of his pamphlets, letters and diaries are in the archives of the Museum of London.**

44

# RUBY WAX

## NOVEMBER 12, 1989

**Ruby Wax, 36, actress and comedienne, grew up in Chicago and has degrees in psychology and drama. She and her husband, the TV director Ed Bye, live in Notting Hill, with their son, Max, 1.**

**Those people who** start their day with some lemon juice, muesli and bran – who are they? They're not part of my world. Neither is 6.15am. I have no idea what 6.15 looks like, but I could recognise 9.30. I crawl to the phone and give hell to plumbers, decorators – anybody I can think of who is connected to the house and not doing their bit properly. I'm obsessive about fixing things – the drains, washers on taps, loos that don't flush properly – and I wouldn't like to be the person on the receiving end of my phone calls.

Thank God I can afford a cleaning lady and a nanny. As soon as Julia arrived I tore up her return ticket to New Zealand. Now Max thinks we're both his mother. Yesterday I had him to myself and by the end of the day I was a wreck. All I'd done was taken him to a fish shop, a vegetable shop and a swimming pool. In the evening, over dinner, I told Ed I was glad I'd got to

# IMRAN KHAN
## OCTOBER 24, 1982

**Imran Khan, 29, captained the Pakistani cricket side in the last Test series. He read PPE at Oxford and now plays for Sussex County. He is unmarried.**

**I wake up** about an hour before leaving for the cricket ground: about 10 in this country. I have breakfast: eggs and cereals. Here I drink three-and-a-half pints of milk a day when I'm playing and find it gives me a lot of sustenance. My family kept water buffaloes in Lahore, but the milk is rather watery. I do some training at the ground to loosen up, stretching all the muscles that come under pressure while bowling: back, back of legs, shoulders and stomach. I get nervous, particularly before I go out to bat. You have just one chance; one mistake and that's the end of you.

When I first came to England at 18, for the Test, the lack of strong male friendships here was what surprised me most. Then I went to Worcester Old Grammar School – it was the toughest nine months of my life. I'd never lived away from home before, and I couldn't believe the English winter. I was very particular about sanitation and had always been used to my own bathroom. I never

## In Lahore, my family kept water buffaloes. But their milk is rather watery

decided to make cricket my career. I just thought I'd do it for a year, see the world, then get on with some work.

In Lahore, unless you're engaged, you hardly ever go out alone with one woman. Here I take a girl out occasionally, to a film or to listen to music, but not as much as the publicity would say. They are mostly casual friends. My family are very conservative. If I get married it would have to be an arrangement. Inter-racial marriages don't seem to work unless the guy's prepared to live in England, and I'm so rooted in my country that there's no way I'd live anywhere else. If I tried to make a foreigner live in Pakistan, with all the different customs, it just wouldn't work. I wouldn't call myself a very orthodox Muslim. I go to the mosque on Fridays. I pray before I go to sleep – asking the Almighty for health and humbleness. **In 1995, Imran Khan married Jemima, daughter of the late billionaire Sir James Goldsmith. They have two sons and live in Pakistan, where he founded the Movement for Justice Party in 1996.**

the fish shop before it closed. That was all I had to talk about. I enjoy driving myself around. I even drive to my exercise class, which is 30 seconds from home. The studio is full of incredibly famous people, like Joan Collins and Lynn Seymour. Nobody ever recognises me. On TV I look like I look in real life, which is nothing special. During the day I have a need to go somewhere – a film location, an office, a meeting. It doesn't matter where, as long as I'm working. I don't enjoy days with nothing to do. There's no purpose to them, which scares me. My favourite workplace is the lobby of the Hilton Hotel. It smells like America. I often have meetings there.

With so much excitement in our lives, I try to spend quiet evenings with Ed. I throw things on the stove in the hope that they are related and usually find potatoes in the oven which have been in there three days. I don't give dinner parties and we don't go to them. Apart from sleep, there's nothing much that's regular about my days. I clean my teeth in the morning and last thing at night, and only shave my legs if I'm going to have sex. There has to be a reason for everything I do.
**Ruby, now a chat-show queen, has three children.**

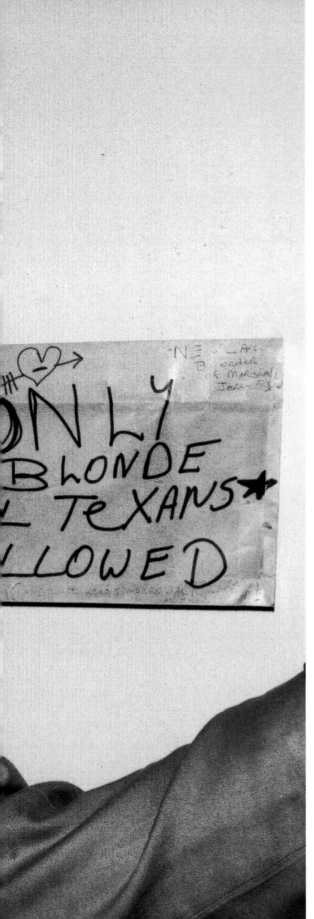

# JERRY HALL

## AUGUST 1, 1982

**Jerry Hall, 25, fashion model, is one of five sisters, raised in Texas, where she owns a ranch. She lives in London and the USA with rock star Mick Jagger.**

**If I'm working** I'm in bed early and up at about 7am. If I'm not, I'm out on the town, back about three or four, and I sleep late. Breakfast is a favourite meal. I have everything – eggs, bacon, sausages, yogurt. I weigh about nine stone and my main worry is losing weight, rather than putting it on. On a modelling assignment, the morning is usually taken up with fittings, make-up and hairstyling. In between, you all sit around gossiping and smoking. I get through a pack a day when I'm working. Mick doesn't like it, so I try to do it when he's not around. On the whole, other models are very pleasant company. My best friend is another model – David Bailey's wife, Marie Helvin. Some models don't like other women, but I've always liked the company of other girls. They can be very supportive. You get the occasional bitchiness, as you do anywhere. I usually react with a joke. Thinking bad things about people just comes back to you eventually. I have various other interests. At the moment, for instance,

# If only rock'n'roll wasn't quite so loud. I stand by the stage with earplugs in

I have all sorts of fab houses to decorate: the chateau in France, the London house in Chelsea, the New York place. And I'm on the phone every day with all kinds of business about my ranch and horses. A lot of my earnings go straight into financing these, but this year, for the first time, I hope there will be a little profit to show.

Coming from Texas, my first love is country and western. But I've come to love rock'n'roll. If only it wasn't quite so loud. They tell me it's got to be like that to really feel it. I stand by the stage with earplugs in. After the show, we go home and I climb into my black suspender belt and get into bed with Mick. The perfect end to a perfect day. **Jerry thought she had wed Mick in 1990, but in 1999 he managed to have the marriage annulled. They have four children. Starring in The Graduate on the London stage in 2000, Jerry received mixed reviews for her acting, raves for her (naked) appearance.**

# SIMON WESTON

## AUGUST 24, 1986

**Simon Weston, 25, suffered horrific burns when the Sir Galahad was bombed during the Falklands war. The former Welsh Guardsman lives with his mother and stepfather in Nelson, South Glamorgan.**

**I lead a** pretty ordinary life these days, and getting-up time each morning depends what I've been doing the night before. In the morning I might go out in the car shopping and picking some things up for Mam. I'm crazy about my car and I'd recommend driving to anyone who's been seriously injured but can still operate one. It's so exhilarating and really therapeutic too. If I lose my temper then a short drive always calms me down. I do drive a bit fast, though. The other activity I find very calming is my weight training. I work out twice a day in my own gym, here. The local council built it onto the side of this house while I was still in hospital. When they heard about my injuries on the Sir Galahad all sorts of kind people with big hearts helped out by sending money to kit out the gym. I just love going in there and working up a good sweat. I sort of lose myself when I'm in the gym. Even if I'm working hard, going all out physically, my mind often floats off elsewhere. It's a great feeling. After I was injured my body thermostat was completely thrown out of gear. On a coldish day I'd walk down the road and come back with the sweat pouring off me. I suppose it was my body's reaction to 46% burns. But now I've got the gym, I can regulate my temperature quite well.

I'm really looking forward to the next 12 months. It's going to be a real challenge. Although I've been offered some jobs, I haven't taken any on because at the moment I don't feel it would be fair on any employer. I'd have to take so much time off, with all the trips I've got coming up. In October I'm off to Australia as a guest of the Guards' Association of Australia. The itinerary involves a constant round of dinners, so I'll have to watch my weight. I'm often asked to do things for charity, like opening fêtes. If it helps others, I'm always happy to go along. When I was in hospital there wasn't time to get sorry for myself. But once I came home I was wallowing in self-pity. It was a terrible strain on Mam and Lofty, my stepfather. I was a total swine, really obnoxious. But that's all over now. No one else can get you out of a deep depression, only you can find the key to unlock the door. I'll also be returning to

With all the experiences I've had, my life is richer than many and very little gets me down. I just like being me

the Queen Elizabeth Military Hospital to have one or two more bits of plastic surgery done. My eyelids stick out a bit at both inner corners, so they're going to flatten them out. I dare say it'll lead to some more black humour from my friends. When I first came home, the little finger of my left hand had been amputated. One mate asked me if that meant that I now had a ring to sell him, which really made me laugh. That's the kind of humour I like best.

So far I'd say my life is richer than many. Very little gets me down. Basically I just like being me.

**Simon Weston, now married with three children, received an OBE in 1992. His autobiography, Walking Tall, was a No 1 bestseller.**

# LINDA McCARTNEY
## FEBRUARY 3, 1980

**Linda Eastman, a professional photographer, married Paul McCartney 10 years ago. They have four children: Heather, 16, Mary, 10, Stella, 8, and James, 2. They live in East Sussex.**

**We live in** a two-bedroom house, so as soon as James starts calling, "Mummy, Mummy," around 7am he wakes everyone up. I like to be the first to greet him, so up I get. I start getting breakfast and before long the other kids are also down. If Paul's recording or we're touring with Wings I try to make sure he's not disturbed. If he isn't working he gets up at the same time. He's an excellent father, very involved and protective.

It seems mad to have moved from a large house in London to a small place on the south coast, but it's so much cosier. We're all vegetarian, so breakfast is eggs laid by our own hens, home-grown tomatoes, fried vegetarian sausages. During the bread strike Paul baked the most beautiful bread.

Quite often he comes with me when I drive the girls to school. Mary and Stella go to a local primary school and Heather attends a nearby art school. I drive a Mini because, being American, I'm used to wide roads, so with a small car I've no fear about scraping it.

If I'm lucky, during the day I go for a ride on my Appaloosa stallion, Lucky Spot. I love being close to the earth. We'd spent

# Paul took me to a piano and said: 'Here's middle C, now learn the chords'

about a year on our farm in Scotland when Paul started getting itchy and asked if I wanted to start a group. The idea of me being in it was totally his. I think he felt he'd be more secure if I was in it too. He suggested keyboards because he thought I could learn it quicker than the guitar. So he took me to a piano and said: "Here's middle C, now learn the chords." So a lot of the early criticism about my role in the group was valid – and Paul himself, though he was affected by it, agreed. But he stuck with it. In my own mind I was giving up all the time – and still am. After all, they could have the greatest keyboard player if they wished.

Because we live in the country we don't socialise that much. Most evenings are spent in front of the television. Before I turn in I always go to the kids' bedroom and give them each a kiss.

**In the 1990s Linda set up her own-name brand of vegetarian meals. She died of breast cancer in 1998.**

# JUDI DENCH
## NOVEMBER 27, 1983

**The actress Judi Dench, 49, and her husband, Michael Williams, appeared together in the hugely successful TV series A Fine Romance. They live in Hampstead, London, with their daughter, Finty, 11.**

**Our three cats** jump on the bed at 6.30. As soon as I open the bathroom curtains, I can hear Sausage and Mash, the guineapigs, squealing for their breakfast. Food for pets comes first. Michael likes breakfast in bed, but I go downstairs and eat with Finty. We love to chat, especially walking to school. I wish acting didn't make so many demands. I loathe being away from home. Something we dread in the morning is the postman. There are so many letters we need a secretary! What happens is we wait until the carrier bags are so enormous we have to scream for help. Michael recently discovered a large bag dating back to 1969. Can you imagine? All those people writing: "Dear Judi, please, please let us know as soon as possible."

I'm famous for my lists, written on large laundry cards – every single thing I need to do or buy. Today I managed to check off green wellingtons, meat, batteries, dry cleaning and Christmas presents. Ian McKellen more or less refused to work with me again – he insists all I do from July onwards is worry about what to buy people for Christmas. Well, I've got 13 godchildren and this year I have 150 presents listed and 18 stockings to make. Being

## We don't ask for much out of life. Just the three of us shut up at home together

such a homebird, I make my dressing room at the theatre as cosy as possible. Getting the nest right is a top priority. I bring in pillows and rugs and knick-knacks to brighten up the place. On holidays we go camping in Scotland and it always rains, which is part of the fun. After breakfast it takes me half an hour to clean up the tent, then we go off to explore for the day. After a nice supper out, I climb into the sleeping bag with Finty, and Michael gets out his book of Scottish ghost stories, which frighten us to death.

As Michael says, we really don't ask for much out of life. Just the three of us, shut up at home together, with our feet stuck up the chimney.

**Judy was created a Dame in 1988 and won an Oscar in 1999. Michael died of lung cancer in 2001.**

**Peter Ustinov, 59, playwright and wit, was born in London to Russian and French parents. He lives in Paris and Switzerland. He has four children from three marriages. His latest film role is as Charlie Chan.**

**I have a** body clock that's accurate as quartz. Despite it, I am beguiled by gadgetry so, each night before lights out, I set my Japanese electronic alarm for 7 sharp. I then invariably wake up at 6.59 precisely, in time to turn it off. Two hours is my personal best through bathing and breakfast to focusing on the post. I usually have to tackle at least one numbing letter from, say, Brisbane, which begins: "Four years ago, I sent you a play my husband wrote before he died..." Under the influence of my wife, Hélène, I think I now begin every day better groomed. There was a time when I tended to dress as if carelessly camouflaged – a khaki tent of a suit from such shops as High and Mighty or Mr Big. I might indulge an hereditary fancy towards fragrances for men. My father was put on a charge during the first world war for looting a Belgian parfumerie. In fact, he wasn't stealing the bottles but merely wanted to try them all out. I drive a Maserati Quattro Porte, seemingly centuries old, because of its feeling of indefatigable solidity, its wood-trimmed fittings

and because it makes a noise not unlike that which I used to make when, as a child, I *was* a car for quite some time. I had to be primed and started up first thing, and changed gear when moving from room to room.

Too many days finish up on an aeroplane, followed by nights in some cloned hotel, and then more days spent pretending to be somebody else.

**Ustinov was knighted in 1990. He lives in Switzerland, where he has a vineyard on the shores of Lake Geneva. Deeply committed to his work as an ambassador for Unicef, he has also acted in his 83rd film, Luther, with Joseph Fiennes.**

# I tended to dress as if carelessly camouflaged, in a khaki tent of a suit

# BOY GEORGE

## MARCH 12, 1989

**Boy George (born O'Dowd), 27, was expelled from Eltham Green School at 15 for refusing the cane. He left the highly successful group Culture Club to pursue a solo career. He lives with his dog, a mongrel called JD, and his cook in a large Victorian Gothic house next to Hampstead Heath in northwest London.**

**I could sleep** all day if I wanted to. I've done it in the past. But I try to get up at 9.30, no matter what time I've gone to bed. I get dressed in whatever's around: trousers I have made for me and always the same shoes. Then I have to get out for a walk on the heath with JD. It's something I insist on. In the past, one of the factors that made it difficult to operate was not spending enough time with myself. So now I find little spaces in the day to do things for me – it cools me down. I'd love to get into all that fitness-fanatic stuff, but I don't know if I can be bothered. You probably have to detest your body to want to change it so much. I like mine. My album Tense, Nervous Headache has just come out, so that means lots of slogging about, doing interviews and chat shows. I get asked a lot about drugs. I sometimes feel I get more respect for not being a heroin addict than for anything I've done musically. That pisses me off. I feel like saying: "Hold on a second, honey, do you know how much money I've brought into this country?" I only talk about it because hopefully it might stop someone else going through it. But I don't care what other people think. It's my life. I need to feel easy about myself, to lead a proper existence; being a celebrity comes second. In moments of honesty, I'd say all I ever wanted was to be liked by a lot of people.

I have lunch about 12.30. I have a brilliant cook who does macrobiotic food: lots of fish and wholegrains. Having a live-in cook was a whim. My brother Kevin stays with me, too. It's difficult having people live in. My only request is they keep out of my way. I don't ask them

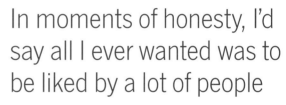

## In moments of honesty, I'd say all I ever wanted was to be liked by a lot of people

not to have a personality, I just don't want to hear about it! That may sound low, but there are so many demands on me, it's the only way to keep any sanity. I'm quite moody. I let people know when they're not wanted around. Or I go to my room and lock the door. Unless it's a good friend, nobody goes into my room. Nobody!

I find it hard to chill right out, so in the evening I watch a video or call friends. My phone bill's phenomenal. If I've got tickets to some glitzy do, I'll ask Mum to come. One thing I really wanted when I became successful was for her to slow down, enjoy herself more. Dad's like me; he loves parties. Maybe once a month I'll get completely sloshed and stagger home at 4, but usually I'm in by 2 and burn some incense before I go to bed.

**Boy George's musical, Taboo, about his life in the 1980s, opened in the West End to rave reviews in 2002 and won several awards.**

# DAVID BLUNKETT

FEBRUARY 14, 1988

**David Blunkett, 40, born blind, spent seven years as leader of Sheffield City Council before being elected Labour MP for Sheffield Brightside in 1987. He lives there with his wife, Ruth, and three sons.**

**I've always been** able to see light and dark, and waking up in the morning is as hard or easy for me as for anyone else. I'm a bit finicky in terms of my habits. I don't feel alive and awake and clean until I've had a shower, washed my hair, and had two very large cups of tea. In Sheffield, Teddy – my dog – sleeps downstairs, so I'll put him out into the pen and put his food out for him. I have a bowl of muesli and lots of tea for breakfast and say cheerio to the children going to school.

With the exception of the time when I went to a boarding school for the blind in Shropshire, I have lived all my life in Sheffield. It is my city. I feel and think and live Sheffield. My heart is there and my spirit is there as well. If I'm going to London, I'll catch a train. Ted will come with me. We get into a taxi and whip across to the House of Commons. I've got dog food there, and Ted's water bowl. He's getting used to the routine.

At the House, I need people who can read to me at all times of the day. Not simply correspondence, but all the order papers, the reports, background material, amendments to committee items – things other people can read just sitting in another meeting. I have a sandwich at lunchtime and take Ted for a walk. To the people in the House I'm a newcomer and they do like to make newcomers feel they've got to learn the ropes. Some people say and do things as though you've come to a new boarding school and they don't see why you shouldn't have to go through the misery they've been through.

I do a lot of speaking around the country, so part of my day is concerned with that. I find the travelling tiring. I try to use it for listening to cassettes of correspondence and so on, which have been recorded for me. People might see me on a train with a faraway look. I'm in favour of technology – I use a Braille writing machine for notes, and the cassette machine. But I rely on my memory. You develop it, like using another muscle. There are things I can't remember, like Shakespeare's sonnets, but phone numbers, I try to remember – it's so inconvenient having to ask. Touch and hearing are improved and I think my

## There are things in politics about which I might've had second thoughts if I could have seen people's faces

# BARBARA WOODHOUSE
## NOVEMBER 15, 1981

**The dog-trainer Barbara Woodhouse, 71, has trained over 17,000 dogs and horses in the course of her working life. She and her husband, Michael, live in Hertfordshire and have three children.**

**My dear mother** believed in the old maxim "Early to bed, early to rise", and I've never lost the habit. We had a very big house, but no servants, so we'd be up at 4.30am to get things done by school time. We'd come home from school, do the housework, see to our animals and be in bed by 8 o'clock.

I sleep very badly because my mind won't stop working. I'm very restless, far too restless for Michael, who now sleeps next door. Most days there are my training albums and cassettes to be sent out, as well as my special non-cruel choke chains. I publish most of my books myself: some days I've got to dispatch about 3,000 volumes.

I certainly love training dogs. I love difficult dogs. I love people. But I've really slaved for any success I may now have. I've always had a close rapport with animals. When I was 12, the stationmaster asked me to catch an alsatian that had escaped, and I've been trying to get on the good side of animals ever since. I've learnt by experience and love, and the use of a soothing, gentle voice, what makes animals tick. I learnt from my early days in Argentina the old Indian trick of breathing into

# Animals or children, the same principles apply: be fair, be firm, be fun

an animal's nose. I've used it on horses, antelope, giraffes... In training animals and training children, the same principles apply: be fair, be firm, be fun. I had all my children potty-trained and out of nappies by the time they were three-and-a-half months. Immediately Judith was born, literally at a quarter-of-an-hour old, I saw to it that she was pottied. And I never allowed my children to remain in a wet nappy. That's the secret, otherwise they get far too used to it. My children talked by about 10 months, and I taught them to read and write and do arithmetic by the age of two-and-a-half. But I've never been a disciplinarian. I'm fun to dogs, and I think I'm fun to children.

But I'm a dull person, when you think of it. I go to bed at 10pm on the dot. My finest hour was when I was voted Female Television Personality of the Year. I was just amazed. I'm a dog-trainer, not a *personality*.

**Barbara Woodhouse died in 1988. She was 78.**

sensitivity to people's concerns and reactions is, too. But there are things I've said in politics about which I might have had second thoughts if I could have seen people's faces. They get it as I feel it.

I've got friends who aren't political and they do me the world of good. I like poetry and reading. I like walking and fresh air. I do some sailing when I can. I crew better than I navigate! Before bed I'll maybe watch Newsnight on television or listen to Radio 4, with a cup of chocolate or perhaps a coffee and a glass of brandy. **David is still MP for Sheffield Brightside. He is now also secretary of state for the Home Office under Tony Blair.**

# VICTORIA WOOD

## JULY 7, 1985

**Victoria Wood, 32, writer and comic, appeared on New Faces while at university and now has her own series. She and her husband, Geoffrey, a magician known as The Great Soprendo, live in Lancashire.**

**I hurl myself** out of bed at 7 every morning. I don't hang about because I'll only start worrying – will my clothes have shrunk mysteriously in the night (it's hard to get a pair of trousers in my size that weren't designed for a yeti)? After mashed banana on toast and a fistful of vitamins I retreat to my tasteless red-white-and-blue room and write jokes all day. Everything is horribly bright except the sitting room. We decided we'd go a bit restful in there, so it's marbled wallpaper in muted shades, like something out of a women's magazine – not me at all. I used to be terribly disorganised, always losing things, but I've had a sea change. There are no drawers full of pieces of string or brown paper bags in our house. I'm very, very orderly. My idea of a fun evening is to sit in our cellar and sort out the nuts and bolts and screws that came with the house. I was at it till 1am and went to bed a happy woman.

I've never given a dinner party in my life. The idea would scare the wits out of me. I don't think I have that many forks. But I do occasionally mix with a better class of person. I was an after-dinner speaker recently, with

## My idea of a fun evening is to sit in the cellar sorting nuts and bolts and screws

literati like Jilly Cooper and Beryl Reid. I did a bit of my show, lowered the tone of the evening completely. The most exciting bit was when I went to the ladies' and found this man wandering around, dead drunk. "You the one on the telly?" he was asking amorously when one of the guests came in and said: "Is this your boyfriend?"

Now the building work is finished on our house, thank God, I'm no longer expected to laugh heartily when a wall falls down. "Go on," they'd say, "laugh – you can make a sketch out of it for your show." After all those laughs, I'll watch Coronation Street on the video to sober me up and hurl myself into bed around midnight.

**Victoria Wood was awarded an OBE in 1997. In 2002 she announced that her 22-year marriage to Geoffrey was over. They have two children.**

# SPIKE MILLIGAN
## NOVEMBER 13, 1983

**Spike Milligan, born in India in 1918, worked as a musician before taking up scriptwriting, which led to The Goons. He lives in Herts with his fiancée, Shelagh Sinclair, and three of his four children.**

**Once I'm awake** I give Shelagh a buzz on the internal phone: "Hullo, hullo, good morning. Any chance of some breakfast?" If I'm lucky she brings my usual: mushrooms on toast, honey, Earl Grey, the Telegraph – Financial Times on a Friday – and the mail. As a socialist I like The Guardian. Then it's keep-fit-and-healthy time. I believe you can train for death or you can train to stay alive. I like being alive, so it's 20 press-ups, 20 sit-ups and 20 minutes on the exercise bike. While the bath's running I switch on Radio 3 and pray there's no singing. If it's Chopin, Shostakovitch, Ravel or Erik Satie, then all's well. Bliss.

I do most of my work in bed, so I'm out from under the family's feet. I also find it easier to think creatively if I'm lying down. At present I'm involved with the Greenpeace Movement, Friends of the Earth and the World Wildlife Fund. Without the telephone I don't think I could exist. I made a count one day – between 9am and 2am the next morning there were 168 calls. And they were the ones coming in! In between I take time out to watch the flowers growing, water the plants and feed the birds that come to our garden. Some of them I feed from my hand – marvellous feeling. Sometimes, when my youngest daughter, Jane, is in, I'll rush down and we'll play the piano together – one of those moments of pure pleasure for me.

I rarely have lunch – perhaps peanut butter on toast and a glass of fruit juice. Dinner might be little more than some pasta and a glass of wine. I often phone my mother late at night, since she lives in Woy Woy, Australia. She's 89 and quite fantastic. I'll ask her things like: "What was the tune you and Dad used to sing in the front room in Belgium in 1923?" And she'll say: "Ah yes, If I Had the Lamp of Aladdin." And she'll be off, singing like a lark.

I'm fond of late-night movies. But most nights I read until the early hours – biographies and autobiographies. I don't like fiction. Then I might raid the fridge for a tin of Ambrosia rice. I love it. I keep great quantities of the stuff.

When I settle down, I often think what a waste – eight hours of sleep ahead; if only there was something useful I could do during it. When are we going to pass this way again? I remind myself. This is it. Use it.

**Spike Milligan was appointed a CBE in 1992 and a KBE in 2001. He died in 2002.**

# THE DALAI LAMA
## DECEMBER 4, 1988

**Tenzin Gyatso, the 14th Dalai Lama of Tibet, was born in 1935 to peasant farmers. In 1949 China invaded Tibet and 10 years later he escaped to exile in a remote Indian hamlet, McLeod Ganj.**

**I wake at** 4am and recite the Ngag-jhinlab mantra, a prayer dedicating everything I do – my speech, my thoughts, my day – as an offering, a positive way to help others. I wear the same maroon robe as all the monks. It's not of good quality and it's patched. I make my confession and recite prayers for the wellbeing of all sentient beings. At daybreak I go into the garden. I see the stars and have this special feeling – of my insignificance in the cosmos. The realisation of what we Buddhists call impermanence. It's very relaxing.

From 9 until lunch I read and study our scriptures. Although I have been studying Buddhism all my life, there is still so much to learn. Unfortunately nearly all our ancient books and manuscripts were destroyed by the Chinese. Before the invasion we had over 6,000 functioning monasteries and temples. Now there are 37. I also try and read western

# SIR MICHAEL TIPPETT

## MARCH 9, 1980

**Sir Michael Tippett, 75, the composer, is best known for such works as his oratorio, A Child of Our Time, as well as several symphonies and operas. He lives alone near Calne, Wiltshire.**

**A new biography** about me arrived this morning. It describes a typical day in my life 50 years ago and d'you know, it's exactly the same now... No, not quite true. Now I don't have to go anywhere if I don't want to. I don't have to work – my music earns its own money. But I didn't start earning a good income until I was about 50.

I do the real composition in the mornings. I get up about 8, have breakfast – half a grapefruit, two pieces of toast and coffee. Then I shut myself up in my workroom. I don't read newspapers, I don't *want* to see correspondence – couldn't care less. Sorry, that sounds horrible – but *not* reading is a way of distancing myself from the outside world. About 12.30 my housekeeper brings me a small dry martini, and after lunch I go back to the workroom and lie down, on doctor's orders. If you sit for many hours, year after year, the stomach is constricted, adding physical difficulties to those which come from using your

# When composing you sing to yourself, you *cry* inside, and your stomach tenses up

masters. I want to learn more about western philosophy and science. Especially nuclear physics, astronomy and neurobiology. I often get up and go and fiddle with things. Charge batteries for the radio, repair something. From childhood I have been fascinated with mechanical things. Sometimes I work repairing things like watches or clocks.

The afternoon is taken up with official meetings. And there are people who come from Tibet – brave people who escape over 17,000ft Himalayan passes. It is painful for me. They all have sad stories and cry. Practically everyone tells me the names of relatives who have been killed by the Chinese or have died in prisons or camps. Although Tibetans want me to return, I get messages from "inside" not to return under the present circumstances. They do not want me to be a Chinese puppet. Here in the free world I am more useful as a spokesman. I can serve them from outside. But there is not one waking hour when I do not think of the plight of my people, locked away in their mountain fastness.

**The Dalai Lama remains in exile in India. There are plans for him to visit Great Britain in 2004.**

stomach muscles as a way of knowing whether the music's any good or not. You sing to yourself, you *cry* inside, and your stomach tenses up.

About 3 o'clock I read The Guardian. I'm a natural socialist, brought up as a proper Manchester liberal agnostic. I read the business page today and got angry – I could have written all that stuff about monetarism a year ago, and I thought: "What the hell does an economist *do*?" About 5 o'clock I might do some serious reading, nearly always concerned with my next work. It will take me three years; a work concerned with Man and Time – oh dear, that sounds pretentious.

After supper, which my housekeeper leaves for me, I have the evening to myself. Sometimes you think, "Oh bloody hell, let's go off and have fun," but you can't when you're in the middle of a major work. That's why the personal relationship of someone living with you is very difficult. They feel a lot of the time you're just not there.

**Sir Michael Tippett died peacefully in 1998, at 93.**

# MALCOLM McLAREN

## SEPTEMBER 23, 1984

**The creative entrepreneur Malcolm McLaren, 37, lived up to his motto, 'Cash from chaos', in his work with the designer Vivienne Westwood and the Sex Pistols. He lives alone in London and New York.**

**The first thing** I do is make a phone call and find out what's happening everywhere. I might sit in bed for two hours talking to friends, then toddle off to the bath and then rush out and have lunch. It takes me two hours to get out of the house because I never know what to wear. I can't wear anything old. I get bored very fast. When I go into a shop I'm the world's best customer because I buy everything. Someone says, "Take the scarf, it goes with the jacket," so I take it all. I'm a sucker for that. I don't go to regular shops – I go to hotspots, like anyone else, whether it's South Molton Street or an army-surplus store or a private tailor who's cooking. I buy fast, on impulse, because at the same time I'm very shy. I buy it all quick so I can get out of the shop. Then when I get home I'm not so sure. It's an expensive habit. Sometimes I've spent £3,000 quite easily. I don't really change my image much. I look the same to most people as I did 10 years ago. But I like to change the air around me a bit, freshen things up. Like leather's gone, over, finished.

I've just finished making my opera album. The fact that I don't play anything and I don't sing is really very funny. So I'm making a record and everyone else is doing the work. I don't have a group – what I do is cast. I take people off the street and throw them in a recording studio and come out with a record. I got into opera about a year and a half ago – it's one of the last places in music to pirate and plagiarise. Because that's what pop music is, it's all about pirating ideas. I don't listen to music much. I don't like music much. In fact, I can't stand musicians – they're very coarse types. Actually being in a recording studio is the most boring thing on Earth, but I do it. Back in the Seventies I got on a certain boat and managed groups and finally decided that was boring and I'd rather do the bloody records myself. I suppose if I'm casting characters I might as well go the whole way and make films.

The only thing I'd say was regular in my life is that I live in Bloomsbury. It's the sanest place to live in London: streets full of bookshops which don't annoy you. At night I'm always out. I go to clubs because I can't go home. It's

I don't listen to music much. Don't like music much. In fact, I can't stand musicians. They're very coarse types

# COLONEL GADAFFI
## FEBRUARY 10, 1985

**Colonel Muammar Gadaffi, 43, helped overthrow the regime of King Idris in 1969 and is now Libya's Leader of the Revolution. He lives in Tripoli with his wife, Saffia, and their seven children.**

**I have a** very small breakfast, a piece of bread and a glass of camel's milk. That's a habit from my childhood in the desert. The desert teaches you to rely on yourself and it teaches you the importance of helping one another. Now, even as Leader of the Revolution, I lead a simple life. My house, in the Bab al Azziza barracks in Tripoli, is identical to any other officer's in the compound. I still find it a bit artificial; that's why I had a tent put up. When I was a child I had to walk 20 kilometres to the nearest school. And as my parents were too poor to pay for lodgings, I had to sleep in the mosque and walk home at the weekend to see them. Today every Libyan has the right to free schooling, medical aid and a house. My mother used to grumble at me because after the revolution I refused to let them move out of their tent and into a house till every Libyan had a home.

There are military things to attend to. I feel we should have enough arms for all the population, so that if we are attacked everyone will fight. That includes women. I feel strongly that women are not being respected in the Arab world. Islam means freedom, equality and a humane society. Some Arab women in

## Women aren't respected in the Arab world. Islam means freedom, equality

some places are being enslaved. I want to liberate all women from the Atlantic Ocean to the Arabian Gulf.

I don't force my children to do anything. But I do try and put it into their little minds that they should serve people: become doctors and go into the jungles and backward parts of Africa and give their services free. But when they hear of America threatening the Gulf of Sirte they say they want to become pilots and shoot the Sixth Fleet. The Koran says it is the duty of Muslims to help those who are fighting for their freedom. I want there to be peace and for the people to end up as the winners. **Libya was elected to chair the UN Commission on Human Rights in 2003, a choice loudly condemned by human rights groups around the world. In March 2003, in return for the lifting of US sanctions, Gadaffi offered £6m each in compensation to the families of the 270 victims of the bombing of Pan Am flight 103 over Lockerbie in 1988.**

too boring. But you can't go to the same club more than once a week. You go from night to night, move around.

The most private thing I do is to go off on my own and design clothes. I've got a tiny room in the backwaters of King's Cross, a little sewing-cabin-in-the-sky job at the top of a warehouse, with drunks outside and iron railings, a sewing machine and a cutting table. I draw away and create things.

Before I go to sleep I have the opera on. Puccini's Greatest Hits – narrow it all down and get the juice! I've got this old Decca £1.99 job and I listen to Madam Butterfly. Just brilliant.
**In 2000 Malcolm McLaren lost out to Ken Livingstone in the contest to be mayor of London.**

# RUSSELL HARTY
## AUGUST 17, 1980

**Russell Harty, the writer, TV presenter and chat-show host, was born in Blackburn, Lancashire, in 1934. He divides his time between a flat in London and a farmhouse in North Yorkshire.**

**My beginning is** the same as my end and my end is the same as my beginning, as the Bible says. The day starts at 10 past 4, when I automatically awake, very depressed. At 6 I go back to sleep until 8.30. That's my dream-factory time. I only have two dreams. One is that I'm on top of something very rickety which is falling, and in the other I'm constantly reversing my car into Princess Margaret. She sighs a lot, bangs the window and shakes her fist.

With my third mug of Nescafé Gold I'll have the first cigarette. It's all ritual. The whole bleeding day is ritual. In Yorkshire, I'll cook vast breakfasts for guests, but I never wash up. I can't stand fat on the top of water or tea leaves. I sometimes dream about tea leaves.

I drive to the BBC, where more Nescafé Gold is waiting for me in a cup with RH Ltd on it. My devoted lady, Patricia, found it. She's my alter ego and my PA. She shields. I seem to go to a constant series of awards at lunchtime, where people like Penelope Keith and Terry Wogan are hollow-eyed from running from one award to another. Afternoons are the lowest point of my day. I am always depressed. I don't know what they are for. If I were brave enough I'd go and lie down, but I was brought up to believe that sleeping at 2.30 is criminal.

I like to be home by 5pm. I shop for food on the way at Marks & Spencer's in Kensington High Street. The first time I shopped there, I was buying potato rings, and at the checkout one lady in a flat hat shouted at another: "Good God, fancy him buying food." Perhaps they thought I am fed intravenously at night time, out of sight.

My spirits lift at 5.40, when the news comes on. Then I'm big into baths at quarter past – because I like experimenting with bath substances, not because I'm dirty. I take my phone off the hook when I'm mixing my bath cocktails. At 6.45 I'll have my first drink – at the moment gin and punt e mes. I have three different kinds of evening: I either go out with friends (twice a week), or to something formal like the theatre or a book party, or I stay in on my own (every 10 days). I go to bed with a mug of Nescafé Gold, a book and the radio. At 11.50 I put the book down, turn off the light and close my eyes.

**Russell Harty died in 1988 after a long battle against hepatitis. He was 53.**

# PRINCESS GRACE
## MARCH 1, 1981

**Princess Grace of Monaco, 51, born Grace Kelly in Philadelphia, left a glittering film career to marry Prince Rainier in 1956. They have three children: Caroline, Albert and Stephanie.**

**Certainly I fix** breakfast. Mothers often do, you know! It's a very large household to run. In fact, there are several families living within the palace walls. Each day I will have to organise the programme – speak to my chef, my housekeeper, my major-domo, the gardeners – because there are always a number of official functions.

I give as much time as I possibly can to my Garden Club. That is something I started about a dozen years ago because flowers are a passionate interest for me. I don't have a technical or scientific mind. People and natural things are what interest me. I find delight in everything that grows, and wild flowers are especially enchanting. Whenever there is time, I love best of all to walk in the hills behind Monaco, collecting specimens for my pressed-flower compositions. I find relaxation, too, in embroidery. My most ambitious project was

# PATRICK MOORE
## FEBRUARY 15, 1981

**Patrick Moore, 58, astronomer, first became fascinated by the universe at the age of 6. He lives with his 94-year-old mother in Selsey, West Sussex, where he has an observatory in his back garden.**

I'm not a terribly early riser, actually. It all depends. Sometimes I stay up very late indeed, you see, and if there's anything I particularly want to observe I don't mind staying up all night if I have to. First I try and clear my mail. I get 20 or 30 letters a day, and if you take your eye off it for a few minutes it stacks up. Correspondence takes up an awful lot of time, but a secretary wouldn't be any good to me. A good deal of the day I spend writing. When I was 8 my father gave me a Woodstock typewriter, built in 1908, which I use virtually all the time. Changing the ribbon is quite a problem, though. I've got two left hands when it comes to anything practical.

I don't spend all my time on astronomy. Looking after my mother takes up quite a lot of my time. I'm also a tennis player and secretary of the local cricket team. I'm a No 11 bat and an appalling fielder, but I enjoy it. My main relaxation is playing the piano. I also compose for the

# Flying saucery and astrology do prove one thing: there's one born every minute...

xylophone. I've just written something for Chester Zoo, called The Perambulating Penguin. It's rather fun.

Despite my size and bulk, I've got an appetite like an anaemic sparrow. Some people are just born that way. Lunch and dinner on the same day is just not on. Half an avocado for lunch is quite enough. But I do a certain amount of cooking – I've got curry down to a fine art.

I normally do some observation on every clear night. Things are always changing in astronomy. You never know what's going to happen next. Last week, for example, there was a very rare event – the moon went in front of the planet Venus. I would say there's probably plenty of life in the universe, but whether we shall ever contact it is quite another matter. I do think that flying saucery and astrology prove one thing – there's one born every minute. I've been a freelance astronomer all my life and I could never change. If I tried a nine-to-five job I'd fail miserably, I know I would. It's the way I like it.
**Patrick Moore received a knighthood in 2001.**

to make my husband a waistcoat, red petit point with tiny sprigs of flowers. I will take needlepoint with me to the hairdresser's, say, or on a plane journey. I don't much enjoy flying but I go regularly to America because I am the first, and only, woman on the board of 20th Century Fox. It is a way of keeping in touch with the film industry – but no, of course I do not intend ever to make another picture. I am not really sporty but I can sail a boat, play tennis. I used to play hockey, but now I don't try to keep fit or stay young-looking. I do put rosewater on my face each day.

I love to spend as much time as I can with my children. I believe the home must be an oasis for the family. To create harmony in the home is the woman's right and duty. Often we will have a dinner party for perhaps 14 people and there will be as many different nationalities. I enjoy it, of course, but the best evenings are when we are just home together as a family, maybe curled up to watch TV.
**Princess Grace died in 1982 after her car plunged from a mountain road in Monaco. Stephanie, who was with her, survived. It is believed that Princess Grace was driving.**

# MUHAMMAD ALI

## MAY 10, 1981

**Muhammad Ali, three-times world heavyweight boxing champion, was born Cassius Clay in 1942. He first took the title in 1965, from Sonny Liston, and lost his final fight against Larry Holmes last year. Now a champion of Islam, he lectures extensively and lives with his second wife, Veronica, and two daughters.**

**After years of** striving to keep my body in good shape it's a real pleasure, now that I've retired, to live each day not worrying about staying fit. About the only habit I still have from my boxing days is getting up early. I'm always up at 7am – but even that is late compared to 4.30am, which was the time I used to get up to do roadwork when I was boxing. I only get about four hours' sleep during the night because between midnight and 3am I read the Holy Koran and the Bible and prepare my lectures. But I catch up on my sleep in the afternoon. The first thing I like to do when I wake up is eat an orange. I don't always remember to have one by my bed, so often I've got to wait until breakfast, my favourite meal. I have fruit, steak, sausages, eggs, tomatoes, mushrooms, toast and orange juice.

I've got two homes. The place in Pennsylvania was my training camp when I was fighting. Now I allow promising young amateur boxers to train there. I'm very proud of my home in LA. Most of the furniture was specially made for me in Egypt by local craftsmen. Home life with my wife, Veronica, and our daughters, Anna and Laila, is one of the most precious gifts Allah has given me. I love sitting in front of the TV with my daughters and watching cartoons, especially Batman.

When I'm not travelling around the world meeting presidents and prime ministers, I'm usually travelling round the States giving lectures. I have 54 topics – the purpose of life, the real cause of man's distress, heaven and hell, the heart, drugs, angel cake… That last one is about the white supremacist society; angel cake is white, devil's food cake chocolate! I want to be the black Billy Graham, spreading the message of Islam. If I had my life all over again I would be a preacher.

Lecture tours give me the opportunity to go out and meet people. It's something I enjoy, and it doesn't matter whether they are black, white, yellow or whatever. If I've got a free morning when I'm at home in LA I get into my car and visit strange towns to meet people. I'm not concerned about any crazy guy who may want to shoot me. I have no bodyguards. Allah is my protector. I am the most recognised person in the world. There's not a place on Earth where they don't know me. The country I most enjoy visiting is England. Both Veronica and I feel quite at home in London. We enjoy the restaurants, the shops and the nightlife, especially dancing at Tramp and Annabel's. Veronica even went horse-riding in Hyde Park on our last visit, while I went out and bought a new Rolls-Royce.

I understand that my fans in England have been quite concerned about the reports that I had suffered brain damage in my last fight against Larry Holmes and that my

# If I had my life all over again I would be a preacher and spread the message of Islam

speech was slurred. The media were trying to railroad me for just one bad fight. Okay, I didn't box too good, but I wasn't properly prepared. Even I am entitled to one bad night. Tell my fans there's nothing wrong with me.

Since playing the lead role as a senator in Freedom Road, I've had offers of other film parts. But I don't intend to make a career in films. Acting is nothing new to me – I've been doing it for 20 years. I'm often asked if I'd like to be a real-life senator, but I'm not interested in politics. I wouldn't mind being world emperor, but it's got to be handed to me. I wouldn't fight for it.

There'll be no more fighting for me. I only wanted to fight Holmes again to give the world heavyweight championship back to the people. But then I realised that everywhere I went people wanted to meet me, shake my hand and get my autograph – no one was interested in Holmes. In the eyes of the people I was still champ, so I didn't need to fight again. I don't need boxing but boxing needs me. Now I'm going to be a promoter – the greatest.

**In 1984 Muhammad Ali developed Parkinson's disease. Now 60, he lives in Michigan with his fourth wife, Lonnie. In 1998 he was named a UN Messenger of Peace, and in 2003 went to Afghanistan on a three-day mission for the UN.**

**90s**

What I write comes from
my soul. What I feel is
the best evidence I have

**ARTHUR MILLER, AUTHOR**

# ARTHUR MILLER

## DECEMBER 3, 1995

**The playwright Arthur Miller, 80, has been married three times (once to Marilyn Monroe) and has four children. His wife of 35 years is Inge Morath, the Magnum photographer. They live in Connecticut.**

**Before I open** my eyes I stretch out an arm to see if Inge is there. We wake early, around 6am, and she'll get up first to make breakfast. Inge manages everything and when she isn't there I don't know what to do. I know some men who live alone and it's misery. In warm weather we swim in the little lake behind the house, then have breakfast in the kitchen – coffee, cereal and fruit. Living together is the most difficult thing there is because it is about constant tolerance and forgiveness. Fortunately Inge is an artist herself and so she understands that I need to shut myself away to work. I cross the garden to my little hut and Inge goes to her studio. Maybe because I have less time left, my writing has changed. It's denser, more concise. Each of my plays is begun in the belief that it will unveil an unrecognised truth. I work until noon and then Inge cooks lunch with vegetables from the garden. She is a marvellous cook, which is why I am 15lb overweight. Ours is an old house, comfortable and homely. I bought it with Marilyn in 1956. Many things remind me of her, but I have no desire to escape my past – I'm always using it.

My contentment discontents me when I know little happens here that I don't make happen, except the sun coming up and going down, the leaves emerging. I have no formal religion but there's a space in my head for it. Maybe I'd believe in God if he believed in me. But we live in a reality that is so difficult to understand. Uncertainty seems to be the only true principle. I'll go to bed around 9.30pm. I sleep easily – maybe I have a clear conscience these days. I've no idea what will happen to me after death. A pale recollection may remain in my work. I'd like to think so anyway. What I write comes from my soul; what I feel is the best evidence I have. Everything you know, everything you learn, it's all a help, but in the end it's only research.

**Inge Morath died in 2002. In 2003 Arthur Miller was awarded the Jerusalem Prize for the Freedom of the Individual in Society.**

# PHILIPPE STARCK

## MAY 18, 1997

**The pioneering designs of Philippe Starck, 48, range from toothbrushes to hotels. He lives mainly in France with his fiancée, Patricia, and their baby, Oa.**

**I sleep naked.** I don't possess pyjamas or underpants – I don't have a use for them. I dispute the idea that human beings are not perfect, that we leak and smell bad. Every morning I indulge in a meticulous ceremony. If it's disrupted, my creative energy short-circuits. I lost six months when Patricia got into the habit of giving me our newborn son to hold while she prepared his milk. I was very happy cuddling him, but after 15 minutes the entire rhythm of my day was destroyed. After breakfast I soak for one hour in a large, white antique bath. In every house I insist on identical taps, towels, cylindrical toothbrushes and the best scent in the world – from Diptyque on the boulevard Saint-Germain. The left-hand side of my dressing room holds all black clothes, for work. The right side is beige. I can't work in beige, so I know when I'm wearing it that I mustn't take the day too seriously. I am not interested in design; I'm bored to hell with chairs, even my own. I am a producer of fertile surprises. A wall is a wall. A piece of wood is a

# I'm not interested in design. I'm bored to hell with chairs. Even mine

piece of wood. In everything we make we must give a third dimension, which is life. The important thing is the joy an object gives to the person using it.

My lunch consists of dried fish eggs from Somalia or a rice cake. I hardly converse. And then I have a siesta. I am brutally demanding about my environment. I could not live in an incoherent place. I've tailor-made my world to be smooth and harmonious, and in the process annoyed everyone around me. According to my entourage I have an enormous ego, but the fact is I live with a gnawing fear that I'm going to disappoint.

My fiancée and I have two goals: to go to sleep early and bore ourselves silly. Neither ever happens. I have the same books and CDs in every residence, so I don't have to transport them. And whichever house I'm in I sleep on a mattress of natural latex with Jour de Venise linen sheets. The beds are all 67 centimetres in height and face south. Once in bed, I gaze at Patricia, stare at the ceiling, and then blank out because I am exhausted.

**A major exhibition of Philippe Starck's work was held at the Pompidou Centre in Paris in spring 2003.**

# MICHAEL GERWAT

## MARCH 9, 1997

**Michael Gerwat, 47, born blind, tuned pianos for Queen and Paul McCartney until an ear infection left him profoundly deaf in 1992. A keen cook and food lover, he lives in Leeds with his wife, Pat.**

**Day and night** hold no meaning for me. When I could hear the wind in the trees and the milk bottles rattling, I was in the world. Now I inhabit a world inside myself. I have wonderful dreams where I'm surrounded by fur-covered flowers, sweetly perfumed water and birds with wonderful plumage. I've never seen a bird, so my birds are my own. They're almost square, with curved wings, and sing beautiful songs, with chords. I'll make Pat a cup of tea, or if the bed's warm, I'll know she's just got up. I can feel the vibrations of her feet and the draught and scent of her passing, but I can't tell where she is in the room.

Before I switch my cochlear implant on, all I hear is tinnitus. There'll be whooshing like the sea, whistles and sirens like a badly tuned radio. It's infuriating, and disorientating. I adore food, but Pat's got me on a diet. She has my interests at heart, but if you take away food, what have I got? The implant doesn't pick up voices, only Dalek clicks and buzzes. It separates vowels and consonants but you can't tell anyone's emotions. It's sad not to be able to share human laughter. Fortunately, I can make myself laugh. When I was having my implant, Pat brought me a Bible in Braille. She thought it might cheer me up, and it did. I just fell on my knees when I read the Sermon on the Mount, screaming with laughter. Life of Brian is my

## I feel the vibrations of my wife's feet, the draught and scent of her passing

favourite film – I can remember that scene verbatim. I can still play the piano, but I can't hear it. I can recall a tune but the beauty of it is going. I can't listen to music now. It just sounds like thousands of cats being hung by their tails.

When Pat comes home I try not to overwhelm her. I want to pull her on my knee and cuddle her. I really need physical intimacy. But I'm aware that she's worked all day and needs her own space. Last thing, I unplug the implant, and if I'm lucky, I'll sleep. Sweet dreams. **After receiving a second cochlear implant, Michael can now hear in stereo for the first time in 12 years.**

71

# DORINDA McCANN

## SEPTEMBER 6, 1998

**Dorinda McCann, 48, chambermaid at the Castle Hotel in Conwy, north Wales, lives in Gyffin with Byron Williams, 45, a plasterer, and her son, Dai, 18. Dorinda submitted her own Life in the Day.**

**I wake up** every morning at 6.30 with two house bricks attached to my eyelids, vowing again to have an early night. I sleepwalk into the bathroom, assault my face with water and look in the mirror. My skin seems to have turned into a Scotsman's kilt, with pleats falling from two nifty little bags under my eyes. I make tea and his sandwiches, then shout the time up the stairs. The response is always the same: nothing. One octave higher: a muffled grunt from him, nothing from my son. Convince myself my son hasn't come home last night and, in the time it takes to go upstairs, I see his murdered body in a ditch. Enter bedroom, which smells of cigarettes and adolescence – sort of earth, socks and aftershave. He's long and thin, so there's not much of a bump in the quilt. I uncover the business end and tell him the time, exaggerating a little, as mothers do.

My beloved, like the little automaton he is, is drinking his second cup of hot water briefly shown a teabag. He tells me about his forthcoming day. Angle-beading, reveals and dry-lining just sail over my head as I wash up, clear the table, find my son's tie. Searching for matching socks in the avalanche cupboard, I think of throwing my dressing-gown cord over the beam and ending it all. No more ironing, washing, cleaning and clearing and listening to the ins and outs of the building trade. Finally, they leave for their respective jobs. I do half a dozen cartwheels and the sound of champagne corks can be heard for miles.

After two cups of strong coffee and four cigarettes I start my own day. Clean the house before work. My life is one long round of cleaning things. That's all I do. A 10-minute walk and I'm at work. First the ladies. On with the rubber gloves and scrub the pan. Then the bedrooms, all en suite. We get 27 minutes to do each room. As I tidy the rooms I often wonder if there are others out there like me, so afraid of everything and everyone, and so humble that they make Uriah Heep look pushy. Sometimes I panic and think: "My God, I'm 48. Is this it?" It's like being in an aeroplane, with all the bits and pieces needed to fly, but unable to make it into the air. I've spent my

I wonder if there are others out there like me, so afraid, so humble that they make Uriah Heep look pushy

# JERRY SPRINGER

**Talk-show host Jerry Springer, 54, was born in London to German-Jewish refugees in 1939. He lives in a 91st-floor Chicago apartment. The Jerry Springer Show has a weekly audience of 25m.**

**I might have** coffee or breakfast. I'm a human being – I shower, shave, brush my teeth, put deodorant under my armpits. One thing I never reveal is if I still have a wife. I have a daughter. When Katie was born, the doctors told us: "Katie has no holes at the back of her nose. She can't breathe if she closes her mouth." Three months later they said: "She's blind. She's deaf in one ear, partially in the other, balance problems, seizures..." I'm happy to report Katie sees, hears and talks unceasingly on the phone with her boyfriend – a gift to all she meets.

When I leave for the studio I take the Armani suits and change in the office. A driver picks me up. I don't talk. I'm not good on small talk. When people call me despicable and loathsome, my answer is "I love flattery." But my show isn't a platform for me; it's a platform for my guests. I'm the ringleader of a circus. It's about outrageousness. We might have titles like I Hate Your Lover!, Dumped for a One-Night Stand, and Love Triangle Ultimatums. Some shows do affect me, like the one with two kids who had Aids. but mostly I don't take it personally. It's not like I know these people. We're strangers. We often

# People call me despicable and loathsome... My answer is: 'I love flattery'

produce shows involving racists, anti-semites, Klan members... They're the hardest. But it's important to expose this cancer in our society every time we spot it.

I live a very normal existence. Unbelievably, I go shopping, just like everybody else. But it's difficult to walk down the street just because I happen to have the stupidest show on television. The job I have requires no skill. Anybody can do it. I'm a guy that got lucky. I own three cars, fly first-class and get treated embarrassingly nicely in restaurants, but I still have the same friends and hobbies. I don't get to sleep much, but when I do, I'm out. I never remember dreams. As for anyone remembering me, I want my daughter to know she had a dad who loved her. Other than that, in terms of TV history, I'm a blip on the screen. **Richard Thomas's Jerry Springer – The Opera was premiered in London in 2003, to rave reviews. Jerry says he may stand as a Democrat for the US Senate in 2004.**

whole life taxiing back and forth along the runway, never having the courage to take off. I'll never see the view.

I come home and prepare dinner. My beloved comes in and has his – mutter mutter, scaffolding, mutter mutter, pink finish. He goes to bed around 10, then I watch what I like on TV until midnight. Bed, to read and sleep, to wake and do it all over again. Clean, clean, clean. When I finally meet St Peter, he'll probably give me a feather duster and say: "Give those gates a bit of a do before you come in, will you?"

**So popular was Dorinda's Life in the Day that The Sunday Times offered her a contract. Highlights have since included reports from Hollywood, Las Vegas and India.**

# EUGENE TERRE BLANCHE

## AUGUST 22, 1999

**The outspoken Eugene Terre Blanche, 54, is the head of South Africa's neo-Nazi Afrikaner Resistance Movement. Recently convicted of trying to kill one of his black employees, he is out on bail pending an appeal. He lives with his wife, Martie, and their teenage daughter, Bea, on a farm in Ventersdorp.**

**The day breaks** at 5.30am, cracking open like an egg. I wake in silence with a feeling of utter loneliness. My wife knows she must not be loud as I take time to get ready for the great burdens of the day. She must just say: "Good morning. Here's your coffee." She mustn't come barrelling and bumping into the room. I would just die. I like lots of cups of strong coffee with no breakfast. I take my coffee black, my women white. My two german shepherds sleep in the room. They are like my soldiers. If I'm irritated, I shout at them to get the hell out of the way. They never sulk. That's the wonderful thing about dogs – they understand me.

I live in a typical Boer farmhouse in the hard and bitter north of the Transvaal. There are always mosquitoes and flies. Farm life, you know, is not just about angels and singing birds. I have some portraits in my study of old Anglo-Boer war heroes, who I salute every day. Mounted next to them is my collection of antelope heads. I usually shoot one or two antelope when I'm out hunting in the veld and then eat the meat. I love animals and some of the deer have become so tame, they wander around my house.

The first thing I do is saddle up Attila, one of my horses, and go to check on my cattle. The one place I feel totally free and alive is on horseback. I feel part horse, part man. My friends laugh that I, the biggest Boer in South Africa, actually farm South Devon cows. English cows. Get it? I also farm sheep and I slaughter them myself. My cows and horses are different. I couldn't kill anything with a name. But I could never be a vegetarian. Only goats eat salad, and I am a man. A real, hot-blooded man.

After I've counted the cattle, checked them for ticks, and planted the corn and sunflower seeds, I write poetry or speeches in my office. I wear brown farm overalls and clothes the colour of the earth. It is stupid to put on a bloody suit and tie. A tie is like a snake hanging around your neck, always sticking in car doors. I carry a beard because I think it's manly. I cannot imagine walking around with soft, pink cheeks – no! And I hate a man smelling like a woman. Each person has his own aroma. Black people, for example, smell differently to white people. I work with black people each day, so I know. I do not say they smell bad, but there is a difference. It's natural. It's because of the darkness of their skin. I do not hate the blacks or the English. But I want to stay a Boer. I created the Afrikaner Resistance Movement because I believe the Afrikaans people have a rightful claim to be a nation with our own history, culture and language. I even wrote our national anthem. I can never, ever, accept a government where my people don't have the right to rule themselves. My ancestors went through wars and hunger. They

## I like cups of strong black coffee. I take my coffee black and my women white

fought wild animals. We are hairy-backed Boers and we don't want our children to be neutral, to be nothing.

It is this new government who is responsible for all these killings in South Africa. They cannot maintain law and order. And there are these Muslim beliefs spreading, which are very dangerous. I am sure we are heading for a third world war. The South African government is sitting cosily with the likes of the Gadaffis and the Saddam Husseins, who are totally mad. We saw Mandela on TBV, standing with President Bill Clinton, and Mandela said people who don't want us to make friends with China and the Middle East can go jump in the dam. There poor Clinton stands, with his red face and white hair. The so-called greatest man in the world being pushed around by a Xhosa from the Transkei! I think President Mandela is an old granny. I can never be false. I don't think I am a great diplomat. I often say: "Just go to hell." I am what I am and I don't give a damn.

There is always meat and potatoes waiting for me at home. My wife goes to bed early, and I never sleep before midnight. It must be my charisma.
**Terre Blanche was sent to prison for six years in 2001 for attempted murder. His possessions were sold to pay debts of £17,000 owed to a local farming co-operative.**

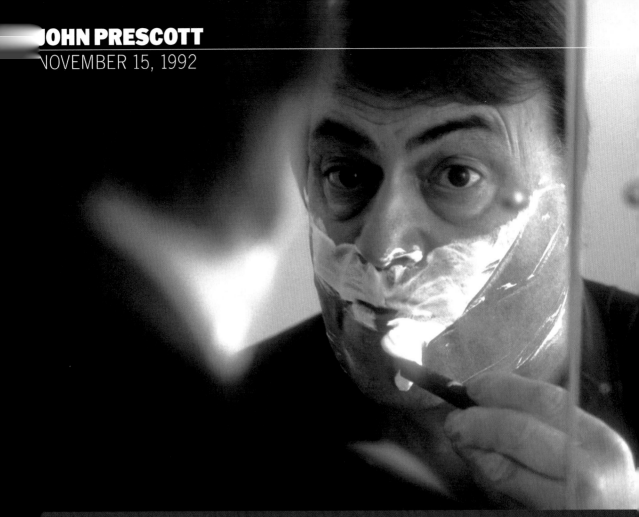

**John Prescott, 54, the son of a railwayman, joined Cunard at 17 as a steward. Active in the National Union of Seamen, in 1963 he won a union scholarship to Oxford. In 1970 he became Labour MP for Kingston upon Hull. He and his wife, Pauline, a former hairdresser, have two sons, John and David.**

**I'm blessed with** sleep – I can sleep anywhere and I don't need a good deal of it. I wake up about 6.30 and turn on Today. When parliament's in session, I live in Clapham. It's just a shell with a bed where I doss down. There's no fridge, which is good – if I'm near a fridge I tend to eat and eat. For breakfast I have a brown scone. I've been fighting a war against brown bread half my life. I'm tradition-bound. When Currie says, "You should give up hamburger and chips," I say, "To hell, I love them; I eat them." People don't think I should be wearing a middle-class suit. Like when people say to me: "How can you drive a Daimler?" I say: "I put a key in the ignition and it goes. It's got style, quality and it's British." I am what I am, with all my contradictions.

I avoid lunches like hell. I feel unhappy with myself when I get particularly overweight – on TV I look as though I'm sinking into my neck. My overeating is partly the legacy of my father, who said your plate had to be bloody empty before you left the table because of the starving in China. Journalists like me because I

have some colour. They turn up at my press conferences hoping they'll get what they regard as an unguided missile: because when I speak I like to *answer* the question. My problem is I've so much to say, I try and say it too fast and fall over myself.

I can't find a way of relaxing. I used to like diving but recently I burst an eardrum. I love jazz – it's a great leveller. You can even accept Tories in a jazz club. Most of the time I just drive myself to total exhaustion and the relief comes from putting your head down about 1 or 2 in the morning. For me it's a short day – I'm doing things I like and there are never enough hours.

**John Prescott is now deputy PM and first secretary of state.**

# Currie says, 'You should give up hamburgers. I say, 'To hell, I love them'

# JENNIFER PATERSON

## DECEMBER 14, 1997

**Jennifer Paterson has cooked professionally all her life and is now one of BBC TV's Two Fat Ladies (the other being Clarissa Dickson Wright). She lives with her uncle, Anthony Bartlett, in central London.**

**My uncle has** one of these terrible things which erupts when it makes tea, so if I am still asleep at 6.45, that wakes me up. I get up, put on a kaftan thing, have a pee and put the kettle on. I feel fab – some people find me a bit too perky in the mornings. I settle down with The Times and a cup of tea. The room's a complete mess – books everywhere: cookery books to review, schedules for television things which always seem to change and get me muddled. I'm a practising Catholic and our family has always been involved with Westminster Cathedral; but they've mucked up the liturgy and mixed English into a sung high Mass in Latin, which drives me insane. Religion worked much better before it was mucked about by that naughty little pope and people went happy-clappy. When I'm at home, I go to the Queen Mother Sports Centre and swim half a mile, then come back and write, deal with post, or do an interview. It never seems to stop. With any luck, I'll go shopping for food or go to the launderette as a treat. On Wednesdays I sell kitsch in a little shop in the Brompton Oratory. Two priests came in the other day and one said: "Are you the cook on television?"

On our last series of Fatties we stayed in Ripon. Often the best thing hotels do is breakfast; dinner tends to be over-ambitious, and what you get is inedible. In Ripon I ordered crab and I insisted on proper mayonnaise – they had that terrible pink prawn-cocktail stuff. I said: "Bring me an egg yolk and some olive oil." I made it at the table and everyone wanted it. The English love batty old women. What's extraordinary is that we appeal to such different people, from children to old ladies. And we're gay icons! Part of our success is that we cook for the home, not dainty little restaurant dishes. I'm a great believer in cooking natural stuff, what God gives us, like butter or cream. We do try to amuse. In our day we were brought up to amuse people. If you sat at the table with the grown-ups, you had to entertain them. Today no one

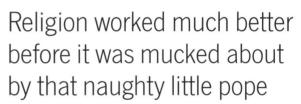

## Religion worked much better before it was mucked about by that naughty little pope

sits round a table with their children. Terrible mistake.

When we're filming, lunch is in the pub if we're lucky – I'll eat steak-and-kidney pie or fish and chips. I enjoy my drink, and I smoke 20 to 30 cigarettes a day. At home in the evening, I might cook a fish or stuffed quails and rice. Also, as I'm rather fond of chewing things, I like making great oxtail stews or pigs' feet and game. My uncle hates all that, so he eats terrible instant things from Sainsbury's. I go to bed about 11 with a novel. It's funny how this success has come so late in life. I don't know if I enjoy it, but I've got enough money for a hip replacement if I need one. **Jennifer Paterson died, a national treasure, in 1999. She was 71.**

# ANTONY GORMLEY

## JULY 16, 1995

**Antony Gormley, 44, sculptor, won the 1994 Turner Prize. His sculptures include Bed, a life-size bed made of bread, and Field, with 40,000 small clay figures. He lives in London with his wife, Vicken Parsons, and children: Ivo, 13, Guy, 10, Paloma, 8.**

**When we married** I said I'd do 50% with the children, but it hasn't quite worked out like that: Vicken does about 99.9% of the domestic stuff. Day to day I'm not a very diligent dad – my thoughts tend to be wrapped up in work. The children are my best critics: Guy strode in just after I'd finished my first large body case, which was 22ft high. I imagined he'd be quite awed, but he looked up and said: "The head's too big, Daddy." He was right. Now I'm working on a project for Gateshead, a 65ft angel with a 169ft wingspan, made of steel. Galleries are wonderful places but clinical, and I've always wanted to make work which is plugged into actual situations. What was important about winning the Turner wasn't the money but the recognition that I wasn't lost in a wilderness.

## I take off my clothes and wrap myself in clingfilm. You could easily suffocate

Unlike the performing arts, sculpture is like sending out messages in a bottle. You never know if someone finds the bottle, if they're touched or moved.

When I'm doing the body-casting, my body is the material, the tool and the subject. Having decided what position I'll be in, I take off my clothes and wrap myself in clingfilm. Then Vicken mixes super-fine casting plaster and dips pieces of scrim, an open-weave cloth, in it. It's a race against time to press them on me before the plaster sets. You could suffocate. The process takes an hour, then I'm cut out. When Vicken digs her saw into me, I shout like hell. But mostly it's pretty bloodless. I probably won't go to bed until midnight. I keep a pad by my bed and I try to keep a dream diary. My dreams are so spectacular.

**Antony Gormley's Angel of the North attracted criticism on its unveiling in Gateshead in 1998, but has become a much-loved landmark. For a new work, Domain Field, 240 figures made of stainless steel strips were created using the plaster casts of naked volunteers aged 2 to 85.**

# DR TARIQ ABBAS HADY

## MARCH 12, 1995

**Dr Tariq Abbas Hady, 34, works in the paediatric and gynaecology unit at the Ibn Albildy Hospital in Saddam City, a very poor suburb of Baghdad. He and his wife, Azhar, have a daughter, Nadin, 2.**

**I wake up** at 7.30. Being a doctor is a privileged position in Iraq, so we are better off than most people, but we have to work hard. I spend most nights in the staff quarters – so it is lucky my wife can take full responsibility for my daughter. Before my daily rounds I join the other doctors for breakfast – tea, bread, and a piece of cheese. Sometimes there are eggs – not often, but we are lucky; 50% of the children we admit are suffering from malnutrition. The number of cases of diseases directly caused by malnutrition has risen alarmingly since the government halved the basic food ration in October. How can a person live on 1 kilogram of rice and 6 kilograms of bread a month? A chicken costs a whole month's wages.

The communal breakfast is when we hear the latest news from the hospital director. Iraq has no money to buy medicines and equipment and we have to rely on donations from relief organisations. But it is just not enough. We have very few drugs, not even painkillers to comfort the dying, and no syringes or intravenous sets. Each morning I wait to hear that another incubator has gone down in the premature baby unit. It is not a question of taking sides; I am not interested in politics. Not many doctors are. We are interested in saving life.

At 8am I start on my rounds. I have about 30 patients in six wards and two intensive-care premature-baby units. Many pregnant women are undernourished and give birth to underweight babies that are unable to feed themselves, and the infant mortality rate has tripled since the war. Everyone knows the smell of hospitals, the smell of disinfectant. But here the smell is of stale urine. The hospital laundry barely functions. Mothers sit beside their children and do their best to keep them clean. This is beyond anything I could have imagined when I did my training.

At 2pm I go to the canteen for rice soup, bread and tea. Then, if I'm on duty in casualty, I'm back at work at 3pm. Around 300 women and children arrive each day, a never-ending stream. It is like living in a nightmare. We can do little to help. For each 24-hour period my rations are five

Children die in front of me. The parents ask me why and I cannot answer them

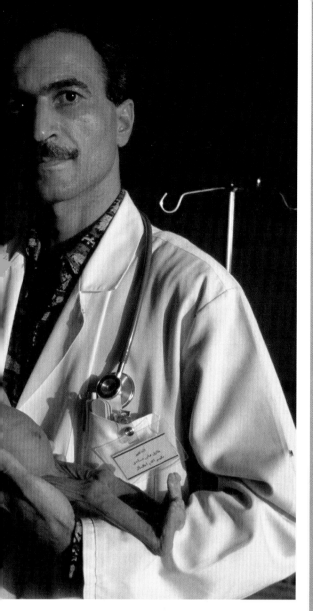

catheters, two ampoules of penicillin, two ampoules of aminophylline, for asthma. How do I decide who is to have it? Children die in front of me. The parents ask me why and I cannot answer them.

Between duties I relax in the doctors' canteen, talking and drinking too much strong Arabic coffee. I rarely leave the hospital except to see my family. If nobody else is on call, I work all night. I am very tired but it is hard to sleep, particularly if I have lost many patients. I make lists in my head of the drugs and equipment I need. And I pray for the embargo to be lifted.

**Dr Hady is no longer working at the Ibn Albildy Hospital. His whereabouts are unknown.**

# ANN WIDDECOMBE
## MARCH 28, 1999

**Shadow health secretary Ann Widdecombe, 51, is MP for Maidstone and the Weald. Unmarried, she lives in London in the week and has a home at Sutton Valence, in her Kent constituency.**

**I was very** aggrieved recently when the timer on my coffee pot went wrong. It's set to start perking when my first alarm goes off at 6.15am, so the smell hits me as I emerge from sleep. I absolutely hate getting up in the morning; it is only achieved with very considerable effort, the aid of three alarms and the reward of the coffee. During Lent, I give up coffee altogether and have fizzy water – perfect misery actually, but it's a necessary penance, and I'd feel bad if I didn't do it. I listen to the second half of the Today programme from the shower. I chat to God, occasionally out loud, and prattle a bit about how I'm feeling. Contrary to reports, I do have the normal ration of human emotion. It takes five minutes to put on make-up and perfume – at the moment Miss Dior – and throw everything into my handbag, so I'm ready to walk out of the door. My mother always says, "That bag will put your shoulder out," but it's my life-support system: two clean handkerchiefs, glasses, sewing kit, a manicure set, assorted chequebooks and paying-in books, my huge mummy-style purse full of loose change, and two pagers. My office is very me. I've got family photographs on the wall –

# In the shower I chat to God and prattle a bit about how I'm feeling

my parents, my brother and his children – and my campaign cats, two fluffy toys, on the shelf behind me. Horribly dusty now, of course. I'm given a huge amount of flowers, and I always keep nail varnish on my desk. I do my nails at home twice a week and touch up when necessary.

I nearly always have an official lunch and I always eat too much. Can't help it. To make up for it, at weekends I eat Lean Cuisines. Politicians don't have evenings and they don't have weekends. I go home after voting at half-past 10. You can't have a home life in this job. I make a whisky and soda, then straight into my pyjamas, scoot under my very heavy duvet with a hot-water bottle and I'm dead to the world.
**Ann Widdecombe is no longer a member of the shadow cabinet but is making herself heard from the back benches, speaking out against hunting, the asylum system and Labour's record on crime. She has published two novels.**

# SISTER WENDY BECKETT
## NOVEMBER 8, 1998

**Sister Wendy Beckett, 68, joined the Notre Dame nuns at 16 and graduated from Oxford with a first in English. Her books and TV series have brought her fame as an art historian. She lives in the grounds of the monastery at Quidenham, Norfolk.**

**Getting up at** 3am is one of the minor high spots in my day. When I first became a nun, in 1947, I was taught a waking prayer which begins: "Oh God, it is to praise thee that I awake." It comes automatically, like a fountain, into my mind, and I start each day with a wonderful spring of happiness. I walk through the copse and walled garden up to the monastery, an 18th-century mansion. After contemplation and prayer, I go to the house for Mass, the great high point of my day. When I'm filming I'll climb ladders, do anything, but I insist on morning Mass. Sister Mary gives me my basket of food for the day. I have bran for breakfast and lunch is two Ryvita biscuits with Philadelphia cream cheese, plus cooked vegetables. I allow myself four crisps each day. Sister Theresa thinks I should eat fish. Once a week she makes me two fish fingers and on Sundays I drink Nescafé. After Mass I waddle back to the caravan, where I won't see or talk to anyone until the

next morning. Hurrah! The library van comes once a month. I read military history, biographies, art books and novels. When I came to live in solitude, I decided I would spend seven hours in prayer and two in work. Now, at 68, it's a great disappointment that I'm too old to die young. Death is a supreme act of faith. I hope when it comes I will have long enough to say a total "Yes!"

**Sister Wendy's Story of Painting is the most successful art series of all time on US home video.**

# PRINCESS SHAHNAZ HUSAI
## FEBRUARY 2, 1997

**Princess Shahnaz Husain married at 15. Her Shahnaz herbal beauty products grace the bathrooms of film stars and presidents' wives. She lives in New Delhi with her family.**

**My ablutions and** breakfast take 30 minutes – time spent eating is time lost working. I order my staff to make sure all the rooms are decorated with flowers and beautiful things. I have eight secretaries, five assistants and two dressers. Sabah, one of my beauticians, follows me around 24 hours a day, even to the bathroom. She is deaf and dumb. I prefer it that way because the servants worship you; I become their whole world. As I plough through my mail, one beautician gives me a pedicure while another does my nails and a third does my hair. Before my office desks are made I get the carpenters to measure the beauticians who do my feet so they can fit under the table. My nails on one hand will be painted while I read a paper, and then we swap.

Family is also a great priority. This morning I rang my daughter and got her to come over – we had our hair blow-

# FRANK McCOURT
## DECEMBER 27, 1998

**Frank McCourt, 68, won a Pulitzer prize for Angela's Ashes, the story of his poverty-stricken childhood in Limerick. A retired teacher, he lives in Manhattan and Pennsylvania with his wife, Ellen.**

**Guilt gets me** out of bed each morning. I'm riddled with it. My next book is called 'Tis, which was the last word in Angela's Ashes. If I don't get a move on, I'll have to call it 'Twas. I write everything by hand – I like the feel of a ballpoint pen – and I work on a board stretched out across my lap. When the words won't come, I still sit there, all day, and write letters to friends, scribble lists – streets, places, anything. I'm a great believer in scribbling. I feel like an interloper into the literary world. Gore Vidal is a new friend, I'm invited to the White House, but I've only written one book. People recognise me on the streets. They're very warm. But I don't feel famous. Strangers tell me: "You touched my heart." And I have to believe them. I can count on Ellen to stop me getting smug.

I take an afternoon break to give my brain a rest. In Pennsylvania I lie on the bed, naked, listening to the river. There are deer, and occasionally bears ambling around,

# Strangers tell me: 'You touched my heart.' And I have to believe them

planning what to eat. As kids, we were always hungry. Now I can eat anything I want, I'm not much interested in food. Because of all the invitations, we've hardly eaten a meal at home for two years. The success of Angela's Ashes has changed my life. I can afford to indulge myself with first editions of Joyce and Yeats, but I haven't time to see my friends. People seem interested in my capacity for humour when things look bleak. My response is always: "What the hell is the alternative? Not all of us are prisoners in a Russian novel." I'm religious in the sense I take what I want from every religion. It's a great buffet out there, and I help myself. It's all a mystery. We know nothing. If we did, the world wouldn't be in the state it's in. I don't like to think about it. Especially as I make a cup of tea before bed. My dreams become a Hollywood movie. Instead of bloodshed, all I see are handsome troubadours serenading beautiful ladies.

**'Tis, the sequel to Angela's Ashes, was published in 1999. His next book, Teacher Man, is due in 2004.**

dried together. On the way to my office I say hello to my husband, Samir. I also snatch a few words with my son, who is a brilliant rap singer, so at least he has met Mummy in the morning. At most it takes five minutes.

At 11am my maid brings me a snack: three almonds, germinated bran flour and some apple pieces – one of my friend Barbara Cartland's recipes. In the afternoon I keep contact with clients and friends abroad. I recently received a fax from Hillary Clinton.

During the week I work until 10pm and then go to the Hyatt Hotel for dinner with Samir. I ride on the back of his motorbike with my chauffeur driving behind in case I fall off. Before going to bed at 2am I have another pedicure and my maid hennas my hair. Before I fall into a deep sleep, my mind races with ideas. I am working on a herbal cure for Aids and my space programme – moisturisers for astronauts.

**Princess Shahnaz Husain's beauty empire goes from strength to strength, with a new Ayurvedic Health Resort on the island of Saipan, another planned near Delhi, plus a chain of Forever Beautiful shops.**

# ROKO CAMAJ

## JANUARY 4, 1998

**Roko Camaj, 56, cleans the windows of New York's World Trade Center, at 1270ft the third-highest inhabited building in the world. He lives in Long Island with his wife, Katrina.**

**Every morning it's** the same. Up at 4.30am with my wife complaining: "It's the middle of the night!" There's no time for breakfast – I just glug down a glass of milk. The Center is relatively quiet first thing. It starts buzzing at 7.30, when the suits arrive. First task is to make sure the window-washer machine is happy. It's a small cage with brushes attached. I do the top three floors: the 110th, the observation deck, and the Windows on the World floor. They were pretty stupid when they designed this building. They went for the aesthetics and didn't worry about who was going to clean the windows which curve inwards on the 110th floor. Once I've checked the electricity and cables I'm free to have a nice greasy American breakfast of bagel, bacon and eggs and tasteless coffee.

Window cleaners are weird guys. I think it's because when you go down the side of a building it's a completely different world. It's you and nothing else. You look straight ahead and everything's normal, then you look down and *whoaaa!* – there ain't nothing for over 1,000ft. I've been working up here for 22 years and now it's just like I'm standing on the ground. I'm not a scaredy-cat. This tall city seems so shrunken and insignificant from up above. It's like a toy town, with tiny cars and people who look like toothpicks. I'm even higher than the clouds and airplanes. When they flit by I have an urge to jump out and ride on the back of them. I see a few birds circling round and I often have the unpleasant task of cleaning squashed birds from the windows when they've crunched into the glass by mistake. Everything has to be very secure in the cage. You can't, for example, have loose change in your pockets. God forbid – if you drop one penny from here you can kill someone down below.

My world consists of windows and reflections. I prefer to be on the outside looking in. I'm the one who's free. Inside it's like a jail. I wouldn't ever want to change places with the big shots sitting inside in their leather chairs. As I pass their air-conditioned cages, I can see they'd love to rip off their ties. Me, I don't have any stress. I'm always having fun and my face is bronzed from being outdoors. It's pretty hellish up there when the wind whips around, though the cage is rock solid. But I've often come off the building with windburn. In summer there's a nice spidery breeze. I'll never forget February 26, 1993, the day Muslim extremists set off the bomb here. Six people were killed and thousands were injured. I was on the 110th floor, luckily on the inside, and I heard a dull *whooomph*. I looked up; no lights. And I heard screaming on my walkie-talkie: "Oh my God, it's a bomb!" It was very confusing. They were shouting: "Bomb over here, bomb

## I prefer to be on the outside looking in. I'm the one who's free. Inside it's like a jail

over there!" There was so much smoke I didn't know where to go down – it took me three hours to reach the ground floor. Women with high heels left their shoes everywhere. It was like a carpet of stilettos.

But I love this job. I get $75 more than the window cleaners downstairs. Those guys call us crazy. They even take pictures of us, as if we were urban freaks. I'll break for lunch at about midday and rush to empty the contents of my lunchbox. My wife packs something hearty like goulash, which I warm up in the microwave I've installed in the shed on the 110th floor. Then I listen to my cassette of Albanian songs and my heart soars. Those are my roots.

I head home at 3pm. I work a little bit on the house and I'm obsessed about cleaning my own windows. My wife tries to interfere with comments like: "You're making too many suds." But my windows are *sparkling*. My wife will make dinner at 8pm. And I go to sleep at 10pm. It runs in the family – everyone sleeps good. How many times did I ask my wife: "Did you bring me my glass of water?" And by the time she's gone to get it, I'm snoring like a pig. **Roko Camaj was reportedly on the roof of the south tower when the first plane struck on 9/11. He then phoned his wife from the 105th floor as he waited for the okay to go down. His body was not found.**

# KATE WINSLET

## MARCH 22, 1998

**Kate Winslet, 22, won her first Oscar nomination for her role in Sense and Sensibility and a second for Titanic. She lives in a flat in north London.**

**I never set** an alarm, but I wake up naturally between 7 and 8. The moment my eyes are open, I jump out of bed. I've driven people potty with that in the past, but I can't lie in because it would be wasting the day. I have a wee, clean my teeth, have a cup of tea and my first roll-up. I deserve to have the skin of a monkey's bottom, I smoke so much. I throw on a sweater and jogging shorts and go for a swim in the local public baths – a mile each morning. Breakfast is bran flakes with skimmed milk and fruit. I often go out with my hair still wet – there's no way I can sit in front of a mirror putting on make-up. Same with dressing. I use one room as a walk-in wardrobe. Racks and racks of clothes stare at me, with jumpers galore, but I often end up putting on exactly what I've worn the day before. I'm still enjoying having all the space and luxury of my flat – it's my biggest treat to myself. I signed my mortgage papers at the age of 20, which is daft really, and I've hardly had any time to spend in it since. I had these great intentions of painting it, but now it's a mess – piles of CDs on the floor, and God knows what else everywhere. But I love it. I slept on friends' floors after Sense and Sensibility, and I'd be lying if I said I didn't enjoy the independence of my own place.

I'll phone my mum, Sally, every day, wherever I am. I was never happier than on Titanic, filming in Mexico, when she turned up, cooked me breakfast each morning and organised things. Mum had four kids, and I want three or four. I know I'll feel distressed if I don't have one child during my 20s, though sometimes I try and fight it, saying to myself: "No, don't think like that. You have to be young, enjoy one-night stands and nightclubs." But it's just not me. I do want a settled life of togetherness and foreverness. I won't be in a relationship if I don't feel it's going somewhere profound. My first boyfriend, Stephen Tredre, died last year of cancer. He gave me confidence. I was 13 stone at 15, and I was still plump when we met. I'm now around 9 stone. I'll never be thin. I don't want to be. I have a very different kind of figure from Hollywood actresses. There were times when weight dominated

**There were times when weight worry dominated my life. Now I just accept I have a womanly shape**

my life. Now I just accept I have a womanly shape.

I'm not much of a going-out person at night. I prefer to have people come over to the flat. The kitchen and lounge are linked, so friends can slob around on the sofa while I cook away. Around a quarter to one I light a candle and have a little chat with a god or something, though I'm not religious. My sleeping partner is a little orange fluffy rabbit I've had since I was two, who's travelled with me around the world. Neither of us can believe what's happened so far. **Kate married Jim Threapleton in 1998 and gave birth to Mia in 2000. They were divorced in 2001, and in May 2003, she married the film director Sam Mendes.**

# LITTLE RICHARD
## APRIL 25, 1999

**The singer Little Richard, 63, first came to fame with his 6in pompadour and a string of hits such as Tutti Frutti, Long Tall Sally and Good Golly, Miss Molly. He lives alone in a Hollywood hotel.**

**I wake up** every morning, get on my knees and pray. I thank God for letting me get out of bed. I thank him for the blood running warm in my veins. Then I order up room service. The chef does great grits – y'all call it hominy. My suite is just like home. I've got a piano, a big living room, two baths, a bedroom... I can see the whole of LA from my balcony. I enjoy just watching people – boys with their girls. I don't have to go no place.

Round my suite I wear gold and silver. I like biker shorts. Real tight. I wear those around the place. And I always do my hair. I still wear it up high at the front. I use hair spray to keep it that way. I drive around in my 99 Lincoln custom limo. It looks like a house. It's got smoked glass, so people can't see in. It's beautiful. My name is written on the back in little letters – Little Richard, the Architect of Rock'n'Roll. If I see people looking sad, I have my chauffeur stop. My bodyguards get out – I have bodyguards 24 hours a day – and I talk to people. I hug their necks and they go to smiling. I like stuff like that. Everybody go to running around and screaming: "I can't believe it!" Mercifully, my health is still good. The adrenaline on stage

# The adrenaline on stage sends chills through me. I scream like a white lady

lifts my soul. It sends chills through me, from my toes to the top of my head. I scream like a white lady. And when I get through performing there's a pool of sweat right round my feet. I've been on the road since I was a boy. I'm on tour all year round. It keeps me young. When people come to see me these days, they see history alive. Before Elvis, I was here. If you look at Prince you see a copy of Little Richard. Look at Michael Jackson – you see me. Mick Jagger idolised me.

Even on tour I keep the Sabbath. And I don't drink any more. I don't smoke or take drugs. The days I've got left, they will be clean. I don't throw wild parties, not no more. At my age, I'd better relax, else I'll be on the floor. In the evening I play some soft songs on the piano. I listen to some strings – some classical music. I can't tell you no composers' names, but I love the music – it's soothing to my soul. And I sleep easy.
**Little Richard announced his retirement in 2002.**

# BIANCA JAGGER
## APRIL 28, 1996

**Bianca Jagger, 46, born Blanca Perez-Mora Macias in Nicaragua, married Rolling Stone Mick Jagger in 1971. Since their divorce in 1979 she has established herself as an international political and human-rights campaigner. She lives in New York and Nicaragua. Her daughter, Jade Jagger, 23, lives in London.**

**I'm an early** riser, usually around 6 or 6.30am. No alarm clock. I drink some of the water I keep by my bed. I sit up in my pyjamas, make any telephone calls I have to make to Europe. A little later, I have something to eat: fruit, vitamins and protein juice. By 8 I'm in a rush. I have a bath, then a cold shower. I love the feeling – it wakes me up. My hair I wash myself, even if I'm going to the hairdresser. I have my nails done every couple of weeks. Whether or not I bite them off depends on my degree of nervousness.

My housekeeper helps with my clothes, but I'm meticulous with them myself. I like to be prepared: my work can bring me to the most unexpected places – to Bosnia, Central America, to the Yanomami tribe in Brazil. When I'm home I do a gruelling workout with Radu, a tough Romanian who makes the dictator Ceausescu look kind. Cross-training, weights, callisthenics, cardiovascular... I feel great but I'm not sure if I'll get to work alive. I am terrified of giving speeches. But I have had to learn both the writing and the delivery. I have spoken on the mass rape of women in Bosnia, gun

control, hunger all over the world, the death penalty, and battered women. I will not rule out that I may one day enter politics. For almost my entire public life the name Jagger has been my identity. But over time, I hope the strength of my actions has established my own identity. Also, I think Jagger is a pretty name.

I spend a lot of time on my own and sometimes I feel a bit lonely. If I'm in, the housekeeper may leave me something to eat or I may grill a fish or make a salad. I go to bed between 11 and 12.30. Though I think in Spanish, I dream only in English. **In 2003 Bianca helped launch the Hope Foundation's appeal to help Iraqi children suffering from leukaemia.**

# Whether or not I bite my nails depends on my degree of nervousness

# MICHAEL OWEN

## AUGUST 1, 1999

**England's youngest-ever international footballer, Michael Owen, 19, started at Liverpool FC as an apprentice on £42.50 a week. Now, after scoring two goals in the 1998 World Cup, he has a £7m contract. He lives near his family and his childhood sweetheart, Louise Bonsall, 18, in Hawarden, Clwyd.**

**I always dreamt** of being a footballer, and to wake up and go into a club like Liverpool every day is the best thing. I'm not a breakfast eater. I train on an empty belly, which may not be the best thing, but your body gets used to doing things a certain way. So I get up at 9am and jump into my Jag, an S-type, about a quarter past. I don't look at the papers, never see them. It takes 40 minutes to get into Liverpool. I find the travelling relaxing. I listen to the radio or put a CD on. I never know what they are – my sister puts them in the car for me. I give her £20 to go buy me a CD and surprise me.

After training we hang around and chat. There's a good team spirit, with practical jokes and a lot of joshing. When you're at a football club, you can't just let people take the mick, you have to give as good as you get. We finish at half–1, 2. We tend to eat in the club. The food's all done by the dieticians. It's usually pasta or rice. I'm fortunate – I could eat Chinese every night and not put on weight.

My parents both work for me now. My mum makes sure everything runs smoothly, and since I moved into my new house she looks after it for me. I haven't got a great memory, so she's my diary. If I get asked, "Can you do such and such on the 10th of next month?" I phone Mum and she has it in her head mostly.

My life is different, I suppose, from most 19-year-olds'. Wherever I go, I'm recognised. The girls scream when they see me. It takes some getting used to. The only thing I don't like is if it happens when I'm out with my family or my girlfriend. They don't want to be in the limelight. I have to deal with it, but I don't think they should have to. It never gets really lairy, but I wouldn't go clubbing in Manchester. It's just common sense. Most nights I stay in, but I do go out for meals. I just would never go to a place that's packed out because I know I'd get a lot of mither.

I eat tea at about 7 o'clock. Our dietician tells us not to eat after 8.30, but if I'm still hungry I'll eat again before bed. I wouldn't know how to cook. My mum and dad do

## I've never sat and read a book from cover to cover. My interests are active things

it. I get something on my lap and watch the sport on telly. I only really watch sport – snooker or golf, whatever's on. I've never been a big reader. I've never sat down and read a book from cover to cover. My interests are all active things. Any time from half–10 to half–11, I go up to bed. I never have a problem sleeping, or lie awake worrying. For me, there's no better feeling than having prepared all week for a match and then running out in front of 40,000 people, scoring a goal and winning. I'm doing something I always wanted to do and I look forward to everything that comes. **In 2001 Owen was voted European Footballer of the Year. In 2003 he and Louise had a baby, Gemma.**

89

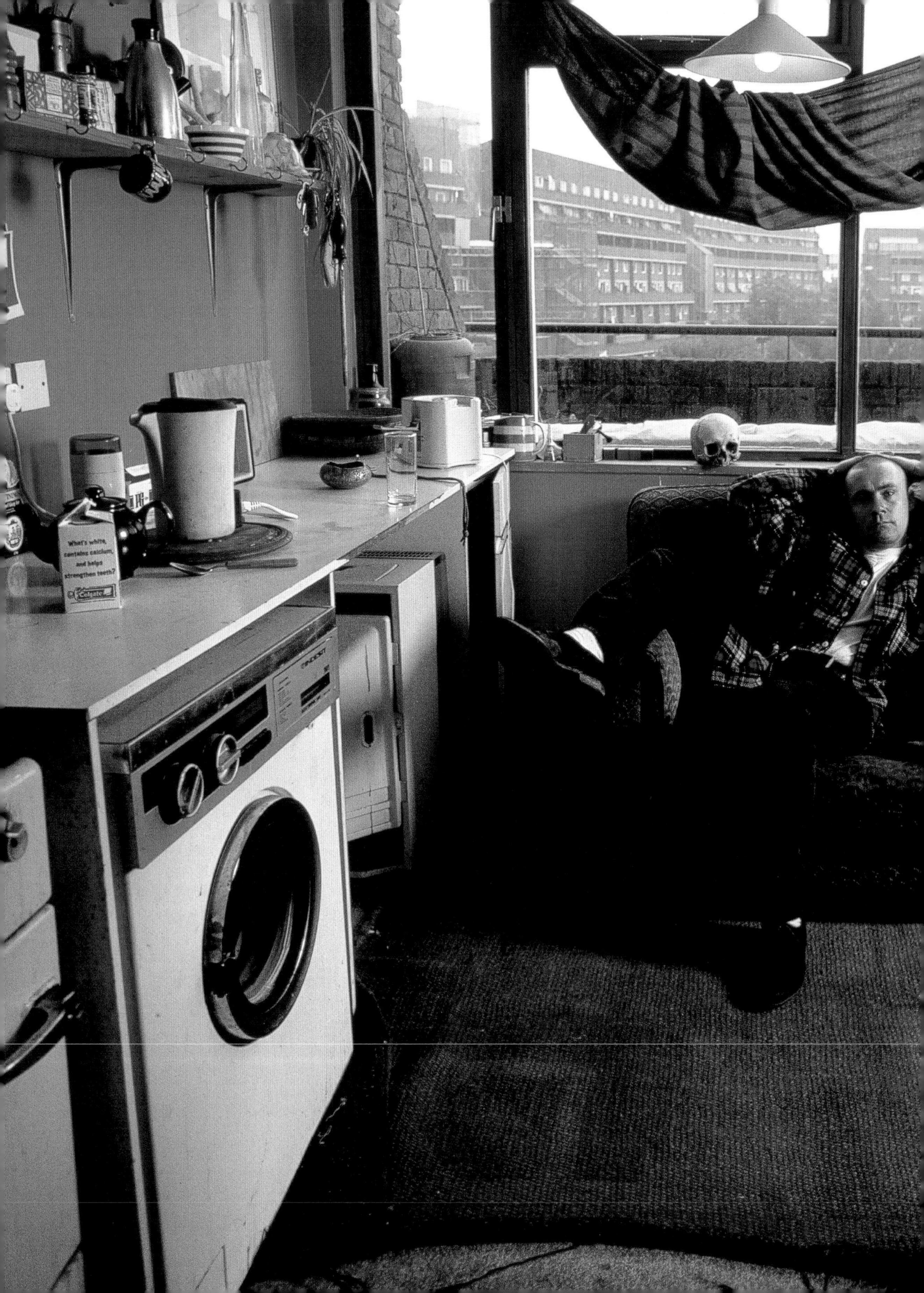
What's white, contains calcium, and helps strengthen teeth?

# DAMIEN HIRST
## AUGUST 30, 1992

**Damien Hirst, 27, a graduate of Goldsmiths College of Art, London, sold his 18ft shark suspended in formaldehyde to Charles Saatchi for a reported £50,000. He lives in a flat in Brixton, south London.**

**I can get** into a routine if I need to. When I was making a fish-in-formaldehyde piece, Isolated Elements Swimming in the Same Direction for the Purpose of Understanding, I was getting up every day at 5am to go to Billingsgate. I became a regular, and the fishmonger came to the Saatchi opening. My flat's in The Barrier in Brixton. People stick these surreal unsigned notes up in the stairwells: "If you leave sh** outside my door again, you dirty scape [goat], your life won't be worth living." You see cars in flames, people being chased by the police. You wouldn't want people in Chanel suits turning up to visit. I can't usually live with my work, but at the moment I've got my two butterfly paintings on the bedroom wall. I smashed one up in an argument with my girlfriend but I liked it, so I smashed the other. If I break something with that kind of fury I always consider it as a possible finished work.

Every day I get a cab to my studio. I spend £200 a week on cabs. But often I'll go out and look at steel, or find out how you get flies or how long it takes for a cow's head to rot. If people say, "You can't do that," I always think I can

# They put up Shark Wanted posters with my number on. The phone never stopped

find a way. Like my tiger-shark piece: I went to Harrods and Billingsgate, but they all said: "No chance. Not a shark that big." Then I remembered this Australian surfer, and called him up. He said phone all the post offices on the Barrier Reef. So I did. They put up Shark Wanted posters with my number on. The phone never stopped.

I'm always out in the evenings – parties, friends' houses, clubs, the pictures, or private views. I always clean my teeth before I go to bed. They're all my own, but probably not for much longer. I've got to have dental treatment because I grind my teeth in my sleep. My dentist says I've got the teeth of a 60-year-old. So I'm having full-mouth rehabilitation. And I'm giving him art in exchange.
**Hirst's shark in formaldehyde has pride of place in the new Saatchi gallery in London's County Hall.**

# JOHN McCRIRICK
## SEPTEMBER 29, 1996

**John McCririck, Channel 4's horse-racing tipster, is an Old Harrovian, a self-confessed sexist bigot and a Tory. He lives in London, near Regent's Park, with his wife, Booby, their two dogs and two cats.**

**Eyelids open to** the sight of the devoted Booby with the breakfast tray. A booby is a bird that's stupid and pathetically easy to catch. They flap and squawk a lot, and get run over by aircraft. Booby has various jobs in the domestic administration – minister of cleaning, minister of cooking, and chancellor. But I've been her Husband of the Year for the past 24 years. She runs my tosh – that's a bath, for those unfortunate enough not to be old Harrovians. Homosexuality was rife while I was there, but nobody ever made a move on me; obviously my good looks came along later. I'm a flash sod. I wear cheap jewellery – not worth half a prawn sandwich.

As most racecourses are outside the stamina range of my tricycle, Booby drives me in our Volvo estate. I've had three trikes in my time – Herman, Hermeseta and Hermione. The Booby buys them from Harrods. After a year she takes them back all buckled. She says: "British workmanship, isn't this terrible?" She's only nine stone and they can't fathom it. But I'm a ruthless rider. I arrive at the racecourse about 10.30am. Time for a bacon-and-sausage roll in the stable-lads' canteen. Nerves take over, so a puff or two on a Lusitania cigar. Being too poor to bet or have women apart from the Booby, a la-di-dah is my one luxury. Then I'm on air. I like to imagine what I'd want to hear if I was a punter at home – early betting news, late changes, market vibes.

Booby holds the umbrella if it starts to rain and runs messages back to the Channel 4 truck. She knows her task in life is to look after her boy. It's not one of those equal marriages. My advice to all men is never make the first cup of tea. Or buy flowers. After you start that, you're on the treadmill. If you take a girl out, don't say: "Shall we go to the cinema or the theatre?" Say, "We'll go dog-racing," then there's no argument. That's what girls want. Women love the dogs. Take them dog-racing and they can't go on about their health. Far better than a restaurant, where you've got to keep them talking for three hours before you get your evil way with them. Haven't got too many friends really. Don't like parties and phoney chitchat.

> My advice to all men is never make the first cup of tea. Or buy flowers. After that you're on the treadmill

When people come round to our house we look at the takeaway menu and I send the Booby out to collect it. She'll have done a chocolate mousse and bakewell tart, so we have them for pudding. It's always a drunken, over-gorged, farting group. I can't take too much drink. I become sick. That's another campaign I've got – if you feel sick, be sick. Bring it up.

Bed is my office. I've got the phone beside me, my form books and the papers. Unlike other sporting types, I have no restraints on physical activity the night before a big race. How lucky the grateful Booby is. **John McCririck continues to entertain and inform punters in his own inimitable style.**

# VANESSA FELTZ
## DECEMBER 1, 1996

**Vanessa Feltz, 34, presents Channel 4's The Big Breakfast, interviewing celebrities on a bed in the studio. She lives with her husband, Michael, and two children in Finchley, London.**

**My day begins** with militarist precision. I spring forth at 6.38am, and I'm out of the front door by 6.43am. I head for my swanky dressing room. When I started on The Big Breakfast, I thought: "Please God, don't let them put me in pyjamas." I tentatively asked: "Do you think it would be nice to wear over-the-top evening dresses?" They said yes, so I get 237 evening dresses a year. I've got black figure-hugging Lurex, rose-pink off-the-shoulder and Dolly Parton numbers covered with sequins and feather boas... The sight of me, with all my numerous poundages at 7.15am in evening dress and dangling earrings, is one of life's tonics, even for me. I've become a gay icon – apparently, I'm the acme of high camp, whatever that means.

The show is live and you're flying by the seat of your pants. No matter how successful they are, certain people are impenetrably tedious, while some are interesting and charming. Joan Rivers was a high point; Miss Piggy, who's a rude bitch, my lowest. People open up to me, but I'm no Oprah – I haven't a lot to confess in return. When she broke down in a show on cocaine abuse, crying, "I did your drug!" I thought: "Blimey! What can I

# My size is important to viewers. If they're thinner than me, they love me

say? I did your cake?" My size is important to viewers. If they're thinner than I am, they love me, if they're as fat as me they're thrilled because I'm a TV presenter.

We live in splendid suburbia, in a house with columns. Michael comes in about 7pm, and we all eat together. We always have soup – the elixir of life in a Jewish household – then roast chicken or Marks & Spencer's chicken korma, or spag bol. Before they go to bed, I read the children poetry or we sing Bar Mitzvah music, which is shorter than reading stories. My favourite place for watching TV is in bed on my husband's hairy chest. If I make myself comfortable too quickly, that scuppers our sex life as well. So some nights he says: "Don't get on my chest yet." I've got some sexy nighties and we might have some conjugals. It's the best exercise I know.

**When the marriage ended in 1999, Vanessa reportedly shrank from a size 26 to a 12 but has since risen again.**

# RICHARD BRANSON
## FEBRUARY 7, 1993

**Richard Branson, 42, lives in Notting Hill, London, with his second wife, Joan, and their children, Holly, 11, Sam, 6. From there he runs his company Virgin, the media, retail and travel group.**

**A kick in** my groin wakes me up. For 11 years now, I've had either my son, my daughter or both in my bed. They come in during the night. Sam's six and I'm trying to bribe him not to come in the bed. It's 10p a night – and we've had one successful night so far. It's money well spent. We used to live on a small houseboat. But the kids couldn't swim and it started getting dangerous, so we moved to this house in Notting Hill Gate. As with most families, everything centres on the kitchen. Apart from baked beans on toast and fried eggs, I don't really cook. Ever since I was born somebody has always been kind enough to look after my eating. We have breakfast on our laps watching TV. The children dominate the screen. When I was doing my Pacific balloon crossing, I told them when they'd be able to see me on the news. Their answer was: "We don't watch the news, thank you, Daddy."

I believe you should encourage your children all the time. Never criticise them unless they're going to cross the road and their lives are in danger. We all flourish under praise: children, staff, the company chairman... I don't really see my job as work. One day I'll be talking to the engineers on the airline, the next talking to Boy George's manager. I've never read a book on management. I just realise people are the most important assets. I give them my home address so they can write with suggestions.

Weekends are my battery-charging time. We take off to the country, invite a few friends round and shut the gates. I love to balloon over the countryside. You hear every sound, even dogs barking. Last weekend I had eight kids up there, flying with the swans. Our home in the country is for the kids really. They can run riot. What money brings me is freedom – to dress as I feel comfortable or to make my kids well again if they are ill. Joan will tell you my principal weakness is women. Since she'd rather I didn't touch, I'm apt to find myself indulging in one or two too many drinks at a party instead, or even the occasional cigarette, which I loathe. The kids will be up until 9 or even 9.30, and the last thing I hear will be Joan saying: "It's 11 o'clock – time you were asleep."
**Branson was knighted in 2000. In The Sunday Times Rich List 2003, he was ranked 15th in the country with £1,250m, a rise of £250m in one year.**

# KAI BONG CHAU
## SEPTEMBER 13, 1998

**Kai Bong Chau and his wife, Brenda, have been fixtures on the Hong Kong social circuit for 30 years. They always wear matching outfits and live in the aptly named Villa D'Oro, Pok Fu Lam.**

**We're like vampires,** Brenda and I. We sleep during the day and come out at night. I studied law at Cambridge, but I wanted to be in the film business. I begged my parents to send me to Hollywood, but they were old-fashioned and refused. I compromised by wearing outrageous outfits and making dramatic appearances at parties.

Most men clash with their ladies, which I think is very offensive. Even the leading Chinese opera stars now wear matching outfits, and Brenda and I are proud to have started this trend. When Brenda gets up at around 2pm, we choose our outfits for the evening. We have 20 wardrobes of matching clothes, all handmade. Brenda rarely goes out until the sun has set. I venture out more often: to meet business associates and collect Brenda's jewels from the bank. Nearly everything in our villa is gold: gold walls, gold doors, gold bath, golden plates

# JEFFREY BERNARD
## JANUARY 28, 1990

**Jeffrey Bernard, 57, noted for his Low Life column in The Spectator, is now the subject of a West End play, Jeffrey Bernard is Unwell, with Peter O'Toole. After three divorces, he has a daughter, Isabel, 19.**

**I'm an insomniac.** My day begins between 4 and 5am. I lie in bed chain-smoking and drinking endless cups of strong tea. I've got many framed photographs of ex-wives and friends on the wall, so I'll stare at these and reminisce, or I'll worry about money or my new obsession – my bad health. I think I'm going to be a real invalid any day now and end up in some home, not able to look after myself. The combination of diabetes and drinking means my pancreas doesn't work and I have a muscle-wasting illness. Twice recently I've been helped across the street, which is very humiliating. My man at the Middlesex Hospital has given up on me. He introduces me to his students as "Mr Bernard, who is closing up his arteries with 50 cigarettes a day, then opening them up with a bottle of vodka". On Tuesdays and Fridays, when I write my column, I'll have my first vodka at 10am. Without a drink, I'm like a tea bag without hot water. I make opening time my deadline for

# Finding a load of curry in your typewriter in the morning is a warning light

getting out of the front door and saying hello to the world. By then I've had enough of myself. I take my column to the Coach and Horses and someone picks it up from there. But my life is not as squalid as my image would have it. I think clean clothes are essential; once you start letting that sort of thing go, you're doomed. Another warning light is to find a load of curry in your typewriter the next morning. But 99% of my ex-girlfriends and wives are still friends, so I can't be that much of a sh★★.

The most important thing most evenings is listening to music. It takes Mozart to give a man a leg-up from the gutter. By 7pm I'm pretty weary because of the drinking. Now I'm old and weak I'd like to live in a cottage in the country again. I could sit and read in bed all day and listen to Haydn and slip away. Hopefully painlessly.

**Jeffrey Bernard died in his Soho flat in 1997, aged 65, after refusing to continue with kidney dialysis. His interview with the actor Tom Baker is on p16.**

and cups on our banqueting table. We have a glittering gold Rolls-Royce. Even gold coins embedded in our toilet seats.

The life of a professional socialite is very demanding. We're out five nights a week; sometimes we attend three parties in one night. Tragically, I'm almost teetotal; if I drink alcohol my heart beats very fast and my face goes red, which is very unattractive. Brenda is a karaoke addict and she's often asked to perform. Phantom of the Opera is her favourite. When she sings All I Ask of You, grown men weep. We arrive home any time from 1am to 4am. Brenda removes her make-up, which takes about an hour, and talks to friends on the phone. I go to the Buddha room and indulge in spiritual meditation.

Once or twice a week we spend the evening at home. Brenda specialises in braised shark's fin, Japanese abalone cooked in goose fat, or sometimes roast beef. I'm a strict gourmet. I never mix East and West at one meal. The food is so good, I usually doze off immediately with my fork in my hand and wake at 4am to find myself still on the sofa.

**The couple now divide their time between Hong Kong and London, where their son, Brandon, is a student.**

# PAMELA ANDERSON

APRIL 7, 1996

**Pamela Anderson, 28, the star of the TV series Baywatch, recently married Tommy Lee, the drummer in the heavy-metal band Mötley Crüe, after a whirlwind romance. She is now due to give birth to their baby.**

**I get up** and put the kettle on so I can bring Tommy his tea. We play with our puppy, Maximum – we call him Max – and then we play with each other. Tommy and I have a great sex life. It's even better now I'm pregnant – I feel at my most womanly. Making love in the morning got me through morning sickness – I found I could be happy and throw up at the same time. After a breakfast of cereal we go to the gym in Malibu on our bikes. I walk on the treadmill and Tommy works out really heavily with his trainer. Afterwards I go to a garden centre and come back with flowers. I love rose bushes and Tommy is planting some for me. He likes being in the garden so much. He knows the name of every plant, flower and tree. He is so sweet and romantic and an absolute gentleman. I've probably ruined his career, saying that!

I have my internet session in the afternoon. I "talk" to strangers and we get a lot of messages. Some say: "I am going to get you off line because you are impersonating Pamela Anderson." I type in: "I *am* Pamela Anderson." Another message comes back: "No, you can't be. Pamela Anderson doesn't write or spell." A lot of people look at my blonde hair and big boobs and think I'm there to be taken advantage of. To an extent, I have been, particularly in my early days in Hollywood. But I've been a fast learner. Money is great, particularly as I didn't have much when I was growing up, and I love spending it. We're having the house renovated and I see the builders at the end of the day to check on progress. But I can get careless. One afternoon I left a few Polaroids lying around of Tommy and me having oral sex. They went missing and turned up in Penthouse in France. I could have died. But then I looked at the pictures, all blurred, and I thought it was the sort of thing newly married couples do. The only difference was that ours were treated as newsworthy. In the end, I thought: "So what!"

We like to admire our house as the sun's setting over the ocean. It shows off all the colours, particularly the purple in a couple of rooms. When you walk in you go through glass doors with hearts on, then you see a drum kit under a huge vaulted ceiling, and a grand piano. I've had the piano redesigned: all Tommy's tattoos are now carved on it. There's a swing above the piano, like a fairy tale. Tommy likes me to have a swing before dinner. He sits there, playing away, while I take off my clothes and swing naked above him. I've always loved swings – I'm like a monkey – and he looks up every so often. Since I've got a belly from being pregnant, I'm feeling a little *too* naked. So I sometimes wear a hat. And shoes. I said to Tommy the other day we should get a swing over the bed. It's the kind

## He sits there, playing away, while I take off my clothes and swing naked above him

of crazy thing we love to do together. People are a bit horrified at the sight of Tommy. When I announced we were going to get married, my best friend cried and my mother threw down the phone and refused to pick it up. I suppose marriage did come as something of a shock. We met on New Year's Eve, 1994, in Los Angeles. He came up, grabbed me and licked my face. I thought he was a nice guy and gave him my phone number. But I wasn't ready for what came next. He bombarded me with phone calls, 40 or 50 a day. I foolishly told him I would be in Cancún for a couple of nights and he turned up. We fell in love when we really looked into each other's eyes. And we married after four days.

We hardly ever go out at night; we're happy with each other. After dinner we have a bath together by candlelight. We're sometimes in bed by 7 o'clock. Then Tommy reads a fairy tale to my stomach. Right now he likes the Stinky Cheese Man. As the baby listens, I drift off.

**Pamela and Tommy Lee were divorced in 1998, after he admitted hitting her, and he was jailed. They are locked in a custody battle over their children, Brandon, 7, and Dylan, 5. She claims to have caught hepatitis C when she and Tommy were tattooed with the same needle.**

# JOHNNY MORRIS

## JUNE 7, 1998

**Johnny Morris, 81, is best remembered in his zoo-keeper's uniform in the children's TV series Animal Magic. With his talent for putting animals' expressions into words, he made Dotty the ring-tailed lemur and Lucy the llama hugely popular. He lives with four cats on a four-acre farm in Hungerford, Berkshire.**

**Percy is a** cat, an Asian cat. He's a very matey boy. He sleeps on my pillow every night. Sometimes he disappears early in the morning, comes back, and then walks all over my face. Asian cats don't worry about where their feet go. I've got Charlie [above], a British moggy, and he's very careful. I suppose he's used to all those English mantelpieces. In Asia I imagine people are sitting all over the floor, so cats think: "What the hell? Sorry I knocked over your hookah, old man, but you shouldn't leave it in my way."

I live in an 18th-century barn. It's designed for two, but my wife died in 1989. It overlooks marshland, and the river running through it is as pure as gin, full of trout, grayling and freshwater shrimp. In summer the cows are allowed to graze. So there's always a bit of bellowing and lowing. In autumn I love to hear the skeins of geese honking as they fly over the barn.

When I go for a walk, the cats come with me. Even if I'm just going to pick runner beans, that's an adventure for them. I don't often have people over. It's a bit difficult for me to cook now.

Besides, it upsets the pusscats' routine. There are cats all over the bloody table. It's anathema to a lot of people – cats on the table. One guest, the wife of an air vice-marshal, flicked Charlie with her napkin. So I put him outside and shut the door. Suddenly there was a bang. Charlie broke the door down with a shoulder charge, and he and Percy raced into the room. Their eyes were blazing, their moustaches were forward. I think Charlie said: "You take the kitchen, I'll take the office." Anyway, Percy pissed all over the kitchen, and Charlie pissed all over the office. They were intent on ruining my dinner party. Fillet steak, too.

**Johnny Morris died in 1999. He was 82.**

# Percy's an Asian cat – a very matey boy. Sleeps on my pillow every night

# TIMOTHY LEARY

## MAY 14, 1995

**Timothy Leary, 74, whose slogan Turn On, Tune In, Drop Out became a Sixties mantra, was a professor of psychology at Harvard from 1959 to 1963, when he was dismissed for using LSD. He spent three years in prison for possession of marijuana. Now a spokesman for digital technology, he lives in Beverly Hills**

**Chaos, according to** quantum physicists, is the basic nature of the universe. It means extreme complexity, a complexity our primitive chimpanzee brains cannot understand. My career has been dedicated to exploring chaos, which means I do everything I can to ridicule the socio-political and individual attempts to control it, both at the public and the private level. I get up around 9.30am, become conscious by 10.30. Coffee, cigarettes, bananas and the paper.

At 11 my assistant, Siobhan, comes. Our main project right now is the internet. I'm infatuated with digital technology because it's brain food. In the 1960s we did a lot of inner tripping but lacked the cybernetic-language technology to map and chart what we were experiencing. Music videos, films, lectures, performances, exhibitions, interviews, essays, designs... I probably deal with more RPM – that's realities per minute – than anyone on the planet. For 15 years I was married to Barbara, an extremely elegant woman who didn't want to live the lifestyle of a crazed bohemian professor. From her I learnt all I need to know about social graces, because I otherwise tend to be a vulgar Irishman.

This house is very human. That woman sleeping on the couch over there is Eileen Getty, daughter of you know, whatshisname, the richest man in the world. She's a leading activist in the Aids situation, a strong, effective and arrogant woman. In the other room is Denis Berry, who's a Dial-a-Wife – no self-respecting Beverly Hills woman wants to go to the supermarket to buy toilet paper, so they get Denis to do their shopping. She's writing a screenplay about her experiences.

Hey, by the way, I'm senile and very cranky. So excuse me. Being senile is like being stoned on marijuana in terms of short-term memory loss. Half the time I forget the names of the people I'm living with. Senility is just wasted on the old. For me it's a thrilling adventure. I've studied altered states of consciousness as much as anyone

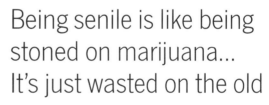

# Being senile is like being stoned on marijuana... It's just wasted on the old

who's ever lived, so I'm fascinated by the changes in my own brain. If I get tired in the afternoon, I'll usually take a small toot of cocaine. I really feel any person over the age of 70 who wants to lead an active life should use some energiser. I never use it after 8pm. If I do, I can't sleep. I do have trouble sleeping. And then there's the frequency of urination. That becomes very thrilling at my age, when you have to jump up in the middle of the night. I don't dream any more. A psychologist friend told me dreaming is the way the reality of your life gets through to you. Pure Freudian bull. **Timothy Leary died of prostate cancer in 1996. His last words were reportedly: 'Why not?'**

# MONARA KHATUM

## JULY 25, 1993

**Monara Khatum, 26, has lived on the Calcutta streets since she was 7. Her husband, whom she married at 14, died in 1990. She squats with her daughters, Anwari, 8, Maina, 4, on Tiljala Road.**

The call of the muezzin from the mosque beyond the *bustee* [slum] wakes me. My bones hurt as without bedding the pavement is hard to sleep on. I shake the dust from my hair and sari. Dirt is part of pavement life. We live with it as we live with our shadows. Sometimes it's hard to breathe, especially now I have the coughing disease [TB]. I only have one sari and *choli* [blouse] which I live in, so I re-tie it and leave with my cousin-sister, who lives in the next shack. We look for *kat-koila* [used coal]. It worries me leaving the children. Five months ago Anwari was sitting on the edge of the pavement urinating when a taxi's brakes failed. It hit her and broke her thigh. She's often in pain. Lorries drive like devils. Pavement people are invisible. We live, give birth and die in a forest of uncaring legs and grinding wheels. At about 7pm, if I have money, I feed the children some rice. If I earn nothing we drink water. The children whimper so I go and beg. I hate it. Sometimes I think I'll lie down on the railway lines and sleep for ever. But then who will look after my girls?
**Calcutta Rescue received donations of £30,000 after Monara's Life in the Day, and she and her daughters were given sheltered accommodation in a hostel for destitute women and children. Her TB was cured.**

# DICKIE BIRD

## JUNE 2, 1996

**Harold Dennis 'Dickie' Bird, MBE, 63, has been umpiring cricket matches for 23 years. He plans to retire later this month. He lives near Barnsley.**

**I have nightmares.** I'm in the middle of a match and bowlers are appearing at me shouting, "Howzat!" so it doesn't take much to wake me up. It used to be my peacock. When I bought the cottage there was this peacock in the garden. The owner said: "Do you want that peacock?" I says: "Well, I can't look after him. I'm never at home." But it wouldn't go. Next thing I know it's brought a mate – where it got it from I'll never know. 'Appen it were Pontefract. Before long there's four young peacocks, but they were too noisy so now a farm's got them, and I rely on an alarm clock like everybody else.

I'm always at the ground by 8am for an 11am start. It has been known for me to climb over a wall because I've been so early. I'm a shy bloke and a terrible worrier. I visit the gents three or four times before a match. But once I come down those pavilion steps and onto that green, I'm completely

# MARLA TRUMP
## AUGUST 18, 1996

**Marla Trump, 32, lives at Trump Tower, New York, with her entrepreneur husband, Donald, 50, and their daughter, Tiffany, 2. Her production company, Angel Fire, promotes 'holistic living'.**

**In the Trump** life things happen quickly. It's go go, do do. Donald is usually out by 7am. He leaves me little notes like: "Be there tonight, Little M." Now he's got the marriage thing wrapped up, the last thing on his mind is breakfast. He's got to get to the office, got to beat everybody. Tiffany and I rise at about 8am and give big hugs to each other while we sing You Are My Sunshine or Oh, What a Beautiful Morning.

A lot of time is spent with my ear glued to the phone. There are so many issues, from charities to my new company, Angel Fire. I aim to inspire people and awaken them spiritually through positive projects. Donald laughs: "Honey, do you really think you're going to make money out of that?" But it's not about money; it's about people feeling good.

Sometimes my life feels too air-conditioned. I don't want a bodyguard. I just want to be normal. Donald wants

## By the time I curl in between the sheets, Donald is dreaming of the next deal

dinner at 7pm, no matter what. He switches on Money Line and I watch Entertainment Tonight, so we're constantly zapping back and forth. The phones are ringing and the TV's blaring. I'm working towards having a family dinner but I'm not doing so well.

Donald goes to bed before me. By the time I curl in between our pure cotton sheets, he's dreaming of the next deal. My mother-in-law bought me beautiful silky lingerie, but Tiffany and I usually pick our favourite matching Paediatric Aids or Angels Amongst Us T-shirts to sleep in. I have been blessed with healthy teeth, but recently Ivanka, my stepdaughter, pointed out that one tooth was tilting back ever so slightly. Now I pop on a tiny retainer just to keep those bottom teeth in perfect line. **On their divorce in 1999, Marla received $2m from an agreement signed five days before the wedding. Ivana, Donald's previous wife, had stung him for £16m. He is said to have around $5 billion left.**

different. The world's mine then. If you were a fast bowler bowling from my end and you were sending down short-pitched deliveries, I'd be straight into you. In my pockets I keep miniature Watney's Red Barrels to count the balls in the over, a penknife to get mud out of the players' spikes, and chewing gum – players always ask if I've got any – a spare ball, bails... So we need big pockets. Alan Lamb came out to bat for England and gave me his mobile. I put it in my pocket and after a few overs it rings. I said to Lamby: "The phone's ringing." He said: "Answer it, man." I said: "You what? We're in the middle of a test match here." Anyway I answered it. "Hello?" It's Botham calling from the dressing room. "Tell that fella Lamb he's to play a few shots or get out."

On my way home of an evening, I pop into the butchers in the village. They make me a potted-meat sandwich and a pie. Then I go home and make a cup of tea. I've given my life to cricket. I hope I won't be lost to the game now I'm retiring; I don't want to be sat at home. Fishing might be nice, but I'd only be on the river bank thinking about cricket. It's my life.
**Dickie Bird is now a popular after-dinner speaker.**

OKLAHOMA CITY
DUB

# GARTH BROOKS
## DECEMBER 6, 1992

**Garth Brooks, 30, the world's best-selling musician, has five albums in the US top 50. While his wife, Sandy, and baby daughter, Taylor, live in Yukon, Oklahoma, Garth is on the road four days a week.**

**I never see** anything of the towns we play. You wake up in the parking lot, the bus starts up, you go to sleep somewhere down the road and you wake up in another parking lot. I bring my own comforter, a big down blanket, 'cos the bus is always cold.

I didn't always want to do this. I wanted to be a forest ranger and play professional baseball. I guess I didn't succeed because I didn't want to show up at practice every day and stuff. But I found out being dedicated isn't that hard if it's something you feel God has put you down here to do. When I played a guitar the result was like, "Damn! All right!" — so it was easy.

The show itself is like sex. There's an introduction, when the crowd screams at you and you scream right back at them. They fuel you, and you get bigger, and you fuel them, and they get bigger. Soon the energy is rocking forwards and backwards. As you go off stage you're physically drained. The stereotyped tour things — women, drugs and booze — we just don't have time for. If anyone had drugs, being fired would be a holiday for them because we'd all get together and beat the sh** out of them. The toughest thing is retaining the common touch. Up until four months ago we used to sign autographs

## The crowd screams at you and you scream right back. They fuel you, you fuel them

after every show until everyone was gone, even though that often meant 3 or 4 in the morning. But it had to stop, because there'd be 2,000 people waiting, and you knew you'd have to say no to somebody. You could sign for five hours and the last face you'd see would be somebody going: "I waited here all night, and you're a piece of sh**!" Damn!

Being a dad now, I'm scared of my little girl growing up and not knowing me. I used to fear old age, but I don't any more. I feel like I've done something with my time. I'd hope for another 30 years, but if it's just two, I can't bitch. **Garth and Sandy Brooks were divorced in 2000.**

# GARY GLITTER

**Gary Glitter (aka Paul Gadd), 47, hit the heights in 1973 with I'm the Leader of the Gang (I Am). Bankrupt in 1978, he made a comeback in 1980. He and his partner, Alison Brown, live in Somerset.**

**After 30 years** of alcohol abuse, I've finally realised I owe it to myself to be healthy. So now I'm teetotal and vegetarian. But I try to put off eating until later in the day, because once I start, I go on stuffing myself. I love food, but I put on weight – if I'm not careful I'll be wearing a bra. Before I start the day's activities, I go to my bedroom and chant:"*Nan Myhoha Rege Kyo*". It's a *sutra* passed down from a 13th-century Buddhist monk. It means:"I dedicate myself to the true meaning." I'm not a Buddhist but I find it helpful. I am quite religious – I went to a Catholic school and have always had faith.

Then I go for a run. If I'm at home in Somerset, it's five miles up the hill from our house and back. I saw the light about myself three years ago, when I was a 16-stone mess and my girlfriend, Alison, walked out on me. She said she didn't think there was a real person any more under all the drink and drugs. I couldn't imagine life without her, so I had to prove that there was. I bought this cottage, away from all temptation, and embarked on a new life. When she saw I was serious, she joined me. But we only spend four months of the year at home, because we live on my five-berth yacht on the River Dart in the summer, and go to London in the autumn to rehearse the Gang Show. I'm on tour in December, and then we go abroad for two or three months, to Australia, Bali and Singapore.

Around midday, I wander down to the village to buy a newspaper and some salad or cheese. I used to be a big spender – now I'll haggle over the price of a cauliflower. I'm fairly rich again now, but I'm not interested in splashing it about because I've got nothing to prove these days, except to myself. Once you've had the 10-bedroom mansion with the marble bathroom and gold taps and the Rolls-Royce in the drive, you don't want them again.

Whenever the weather permits, I spend the afternoon on my boat. I bought it when I gave up booze and it's been very good for me. We'll sail down to Dartmouth, go ashore in the dinghy for lunch, and then go back to the boat and play Scrabble. Alison and I play Scrabble everywhere, even outside restaurants. It's a great way to

My girlfriend said she didn't think there was a real person any more under all the drink and drugs

# SOCKS
## OCTOBER 20, 1996

**Socks, 5, America's First Cat, takes his name from his distinctive white paws. Rescued as a stray in Little Rock, Arkansas, he moved into the White House with the Clinton family in 1992.**

**I sleep in** this little hideaway I've found in the basement of my big white house. Around 5.30am I do a couple of slow stretches, then mosey on up to the family quarters to snuggle down on Chelsea's bed. By the time she wakes I'm pretty hungry, so I'm off to check out my bowl. I'm mainly a Fancy Feast guy.

For most of the morning I stay on the South Lawn. I don't have much choice: I've been put on a leash ever since a bunch of Bill's muscle-bound minders tripped over me. But there's a good deal of slack for prowling and I've found this great place near the rose garden where I sit and do my grooming. I never eat the grass – that's a foul habit. I did chew a little back in Little Rock, but I never swallowed.

Some days, Bill or Hillary will see me on their way out somewhere and we'll share some quality petting time. Then early afternoon I swing by my buddy Neel [Lattimore], Hillary's press officer, and paw over the mail. I get so many letters Neel had to get a special staff together to answer them. The Washington Times ran a story, and Bill had to answer questions about how much my fan club was costing taxpayers. There have

## I never eat grass. I did chew a little once, but I never swallowed

been cartoons, T-shirts, mugs, a video game. Now I'm supposed to have written a book, Socks Goes to Washington: The Diary of America's First Cat. Purr-lease! I think anthropomorphism is sick. Some people think it's cute to speak for me in a squeaky voice. They say things like: "Now, where did I leave Mister Mousey?" I wish I could speak for them and say something like: "Hi, I've just had a lobotomy."

If there are a lot of feet scurrying about, it means there's a state banquet, and I hightail it back to the basement. Frankly, I'm beat by 8.30pm. I finish any leftovers in my bowl and sneak off for some sleep. I've been having this recurring nightmare in which I'm not re-inaugurated and have to make way for Bob and Liddy Dole's tank of rare tropical fish. Fat chance.

**When the Clintons left the White House in January 2001, Socks was adopted by one of his favourite humans, Betty Currie, the ex-president's personal secretary.**

make friends. I chant again for 10 minutes in the evening. If I'm in the mood, I'll wear sequins. The best evening of all is a get-together with my Uncle John, my brother, Tony, who sings in pubs and clubs, and my son and daughter. We sit around and sing and play guitars. They all sing better than I do – but at least I look the part.

**Glitter lives in exile, having served half of a four-month jail sentence in 1999 after admitting 54 charges of possessing child pornography downloaded from the internet. It included images of girls as young as 2 being abused. Since his release from prison, Glitter has been expelled from Cuba and requested to leave Cambodia.**

**Mark Harris, 26, works as a body piercer, in Soho, London. His list of high-profile clients includes Scary Spice and Brad Pitt, as well as judges and priests. Divorced, he lives alone in Brixton, south London.**

**I wake laughing.** I've just bought a mad crab alarm clock which vibrates and wobbles and makes stupid noises. I'm a very happy person. When I had my left hand tattooed, I woke up to see this scary thing waving about in front of my face. It was as if it didn't belong to me; it still isn't really mine, but it's so beautiful, it kills me. I can't stop looking at it.

I get questions about body piercing from all over the world, so first thing I'll switch on the laptop to see if there's any e-mail. Then I make toast and coffee and get into a candlelit bath sprinkled with tea-tree oil. It really chills me out. I've always lived with girlfriends and I'm enjoying having my own place. My hall's red and there's a huge painting of the Madonna and Child. I've got her tattooed on my back, too – it's the most powerful image I can think of, partly because I'm a lapsed Catholic boy, but also because I'm very close to my mother. She's my No 1 girl and I adore her.

I've been into piercing since I was small. My biggest influence was National Geographic magazine. I used to study the pictures of African women with neck rings and lip plates. I studied anatomy and read loads of technical books before I started piercing other people. You have to know what you're doing. If you pierce a section of umbilicus, you're in trouble. During my first piercing, I got such a rush I had to leave the room – it was a feeling of pure euphoria, and I still get that when I'm piercing special friends. It's like giving someone a gift.

I'm tattooed from my knees to my feet and over my bum and up my back to my neck. My arms are a mixture of Marquesian and Polynesian tribal markings. I made a commitment to myself about six months ago to go all the way. I feel you're born with a blank canvas and you're free to do what you want with it.

My oldest client is 89 and I've got about 50 regulars: judges, barristers, priests. One priest comes a lot; he's got a genital ring and I've just pierced his nipples. And I can't listen to Question Time without laughing, because I know how many of the MPs are pierced under their suits. Before I start, I clean my room – surfaces, floors, everything. The clamps have all been autoclaved the night before and they go from there into ultrasonic, so they're completely sterile. I never use a gun – they can carry HIV and hepatitis B and C. Also, a gun spreads the cartilage, whereas a hollow needle allows a section of skin to be removed. People should be more worried about HIV – there are so many dodgy piercers and tattooists. I'm careful to the point of obsession about hygiene. One of the most popular rings is a Prince Albert. Loads of Victorian gents, like Albert, had genital rings; they wore

## You're born with a blank canvas and you're free to do what you want with it

incredibly tight breeches and they didn't want unsightly bulges. A Prince Albert is threaded through the urethra like a catheter, to the flare of the penis, then it pierces the fraenum and comes out underneath. They'd tie a chain to it and hang a little weight on the end. It made the penis hang to one side or the other, and ensured a smooth line. Piercing's a beautiful experience. I had mine done lying on cushions on the floor, with candles burning and tranquil music. It's like a ritual initiation. People are often nervous – you talk them down to a state of calmness and trust.

I go to The Stockpot for lunch – gammon steak, eggs, chips and vegetables for £3.50. The only thing I can't eat is spaghetti. It gets wound round the stud in my tongue. It doesn't hurt; all the nerve endings and tastebuds are around the outside. But I have to go to the dentist a lot – the metal's starting to knock the enamel off my teeth.

I don't go out much in the evening. I'm too tired. I play music and have another bath. What I love is to get into a bed made up with clean white sheets. My girlfriend comes over a couple of times a week, but I like sleeping alone. I need my space. All I've ever wanted is to be a free person, to do what I do and not be judged for it. I'm like a chameleon, changing colour.
**Mark Harris's present whereabouts are unknown.**

# PEDRO ALMODOVAR

## MARCH 24, 1996

**Pedro Almodóvar, born in La Mancha in 1949, has directed 11 films in the past 15 years. In three of them, his mother, Francisca Caballera (left), has played cameo roles. He lives alone in Madrid.**

**Sometimes I wake** up wishing I could be someone else. I am bored with being Pedro Almodóvar. I fantasise about using a pseudonym: Harry Cane – if you say it quickly it sounds like hurricane. Anyway, my brother, Agustín, has forbidden me. We run our production company, El Deseo, together. He says it took us long enough to get where we are, we're not starting again. In Madrid people treat me as if I were a neighbour to the whole nation. Everybody comes up, saying: "How's it going? God bless you." It's really great. They don't treat me with the respect they would somebody they thought was really important. If I'm not shooting, I often go to our offices, but I can only write at home. I need to be by myself. Solitude can be very productive. I feel I'm master of my solitude. I use it. At the moment, I am writing three films; they completely absorb me. I become almost autistic. The best relief from solitude is the cinema. It is always a passion. It's like being in love. Usually I go alone. I'll just think: "I've got a couple of hours. I'll go now."

I don't find nightlife as entertaining as I used to. When I do go out, I feel I'm repeating a situation I already know. I have never drunk and I don't take drugs any more. I only drink water. But I would like to go out more often, just to listen to people's conversations. I am very curious. I'd like

## The best relief from solitude is the cinema. It is always a passion, like being in love

to overhear more young people, 15-to-20-year-olds. They are completely different from us.

If I'm engrossed in something I can stay up all night. I love women's tennis and would stay awake to watch Arantxa Sánchez finish a match. Sport also represents a pleasure I can't have. As I'd like to experience all pleasures, it's both fascinating and frustrating. Most nights, I dream of a story I'd like to write or a favourite scene from an old film, shot in a different genre and directed by me.

**In 2003 Pedro Almodóvar won his first Academy Award (best original screenplay) for Talk to Her.**

# JEANNE CALMENT

## MAY 26, 1996

**Jeanne Calment, thought to be the world's oldest living person, was born in 1875. She was 44 when French women won the vote. Blind and nearly deaf, she lives in a retirement home in Arles, Provence.**

**I can no** longer see, but I am aware of the changing rhythms, the difference in texture between day and night. I wake at 8am with a sense of pleasure that it's a new day. Breakfast is chocolate or vanilla porridge with a knob of butter. I am fed by a minder, then dressed and combed. I am very *coquette* and it's important for me to be well groomed. Once I had grand furs and satin dresses. My deafness isolates me but I never allow myself to get depressed. I can live on my past, rewinding images in my mind. I remember when the Eiffel Tower was being built. I went there for my honeymoon in 1896 and I climbed to the top. When I married my cousin, Fernand, it was a great event. He died during the second world war, poisoned by infected cherries. I would hunt boar with him and he would complain I wasn't timid enough. *Oh la la*! But I am not afraid of anything. I met Van Gogh once. He was completely crazy. His brain was pickled by alcohol – you could smell it on his breath. His hair was wild and he was rough and impolite. But he painted beautifully.

At 6.30pm I have five spoons of soup. I count them ... one, two, three, four, five. Then five spoons of dessert. I'm in bed by 8pm in my hospital nightshirt. People ask me if I am tired. Tired? That is not the word, I am indefatigable. I don't believe in an afterlife. But one must always smile. I think I will die smiling. Death doesn't scare me. I go to bed peacefully. And I sleep like a baby. Like a baby!
**Jeanne Calment died in 1997 at the age of 122.**

# BAYSEE ROWE

## JULY 2, 1995

**The bus conductor Baysee Rowe, 29, sings to his passengers on London's 38 route from Victoria to Clapton Pond. His first single, Sugar Sugar, released on his own Double Decker label, reached No 30. He lives on his own in Leyton.**

**We get a** new uniform every seven months; I wear my own boots with red, yellow and green laces to show I'm ragamuffin. Under the uniform I'm a free spirit. I love people, I love reggae music. I used to wear a bandanna and the inspectors gave me hell. I'd take it off, then put it on again once we'd gone round the corner. They'd radio through to the bus station at Victoria, saying: "He's still got that thing on his head."

On a Monday, nobody talks. But I try and make an effort. We've had nine assaults on my route but no one's ever gone for me. If there's any sign of trouble I just start singing madly. Some duties are spread-overs; 12-hour shifts with a four-hour interval in the middle. I like them because if I've had an idea for a song standing on the platform in the morning, I've got time to go home and record it before I go back.

# DAVID HELFGOTT

## MAY 4, 1997

**David Helfgott, 49, inspired the Oscar-winning film Shine. Born in Melbourne, he was disowned by his father for leaving home to study music. He spent 10 years in psychiatric institutions before marrying Gillian, 53, and resuming his career. They live in The Promised Land, Bellingen, New South Wales**

**I wake joyeux** about 6.30. I leap out of bed, run around, do my dentifies [teeth]. I like soft, comfy clothes, but less is better and naked is best of all. Gillian buys clothes for me: shops are pretty awesome – you've got to be very fit to go shopping. I should have a shower straightaway, but usually I don't, though I have plenteous showers and swims every day, wherever I am in the world. I'll make the bed, peg out the washing, sweep the kitchen and the paths, do the dishes. And I'll write my composodlies [compositions] and cuddle Gillian and give her plenteous potchnagoolas [kisses]. She means the world to me. Living with me can be hell. I can never find anything in the cupboards, or where I put my music. I talk a lot, too, so Gillian doesn't get much peace. Our home in The Promised Land is beautiful. My favourite thing is the

## I'll write my composodlies, cuddle Gillian and give her plenteous potchnagoolas

grand piano, given to me by friends. A miracle! Pianos are my best friends. I'll practise for five or six hours a day. The Rach 3 is very special to me. It's awesome, vast like the sea. Of course, playing the piano is a risky business, but you gotta take risks because life is a short trick. My life should have been different. My father said: "You thought you were so smart. You thought you'd go from one concert hall to another. Well, you'll only be going from one hospital to another." He made a huge mistake but perhaps he loved me too much, loved me to bits and pieces. It was a shamus, really. But one has to forgive and enjoy the now. I enjoy having money, and people come up to me wherever I go. I'm no longer scared – I love them talking to me. And you shouldn't get scared. We have a lot of soirées at home and I play to our friends. I go to bed about 11pm. I still dream about music. I'm very privileged. Gotta be grateful. **In 1997 David fulfilled his dream of performing 'Rach 3' at the Albert Hall. After giving concerts around the globe, he hopes to semi–retire in 2004.**

I'm not too bothered about food. I only use my kitchen for sampling. I record running water or sizzling oil, put it into the sampling machine and use it like a note. My flat is basically a recording studio. I have £15,000 worth of recording equipment – bought piece by piece – but no washing machine or bed. It doesn't bother me. I don't have much of a social life, but I don't get lonely. Music is the best wife you could have, she never argues and she always pleases.

I don't want to give up the buses; not only does it pay my mortgage but I like it. I had a letter from the chief executive saying: "I would like to thank you for being such a wonderful ambassador for our company." It brought tears to my eyes. People say: "You should go to America and make lots of money." But England is the only country which still has bus conductors, and I'm the singing conductor.
**Baysee Rowe still conducts and entertains customers on the No 38 bus. He regularly appears at music festivals around the country and has set up a new record label, Send Records, through which he is planning to release an album, The Confessions of a Conductor.**

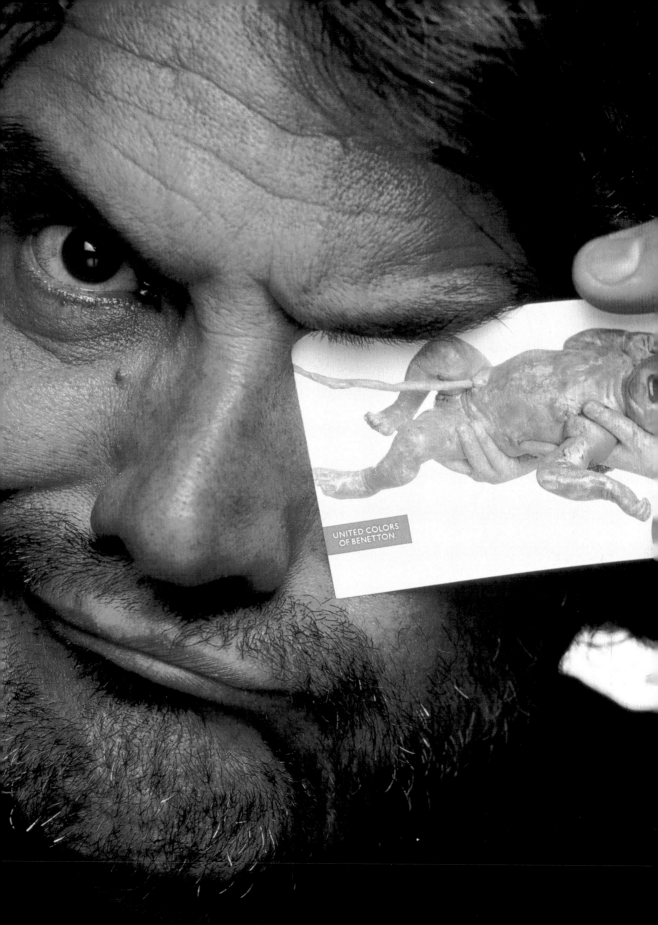

UNITED COLORS
OF BENETTON.

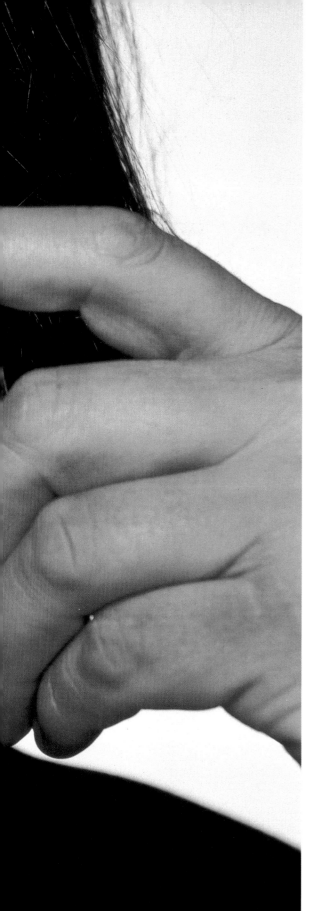

# OLIVIERO TOSCANI

## OCTOBER 15, 1995

**Oliviero Toscani's advertising images for Benetton – an Aids patient, a priest kissing a nun, and a newborn baby – have led to controversy and legal action. Aged 53, he lives in Tuscany with his family.**

**Because I'm excited** about what I do I wake up with a natural jolt, at 5am. I have horses, cows, chickens and a vegetable garden, so I can be completely independent from the world. We can live off our own food and wine – it's a psychological thing. I drive a Land Rover because I love English cars. They're like unfaithful girlfriends: they let you down, but they do have incredible charisma. After taking my daughter to school, I ride my Appaloosa ponies. My wooden horseboxes are made in England – not even the Queen has hers made in wood. I suspect the English like animals more than humans. My photograph of a baby with its umbilical cord was banned – they cried: "Shocking! Shocking! So bloody!" It's my favourite. I set up a studio in the delivery room and they dressed me like a doctor. When the baby was born I had two seconds – two clicks, and that was it. Actually I like criticism; at least it means people are looking at my work. I'm not a genius,

## I'm not a genius. It's just that I am not retarded like other advertising people

it's just that I'm not retarded like other advertising people.

I'm very disciplined and a bell rings at 1pm to signal the family to lunch. Everything tastes better because it's produced at home. I travel frequently, taking photographs and directing Colors, the magazine Benetton sponsors. I never go on vacation – my life is a vacation. It may sound idyllic, but when you recognise you are privileged, you are more sensitive to global trauma.

In the evening, the bell rings and we eat in the kitchen with the children. We don't own a television set. I really hate television. It's more a dictatorship; it's worse than Hitler. The kids go to bed between 8 and 9pm and then Kirsti and I sit on the veranda looking at the view. I've got a smart woman. She is above career, power and feminism. And she understands the basic thing: I need to be loved. **In 2002 Toscani sparked a furore with his poster, depicting a crucifix merged with a swastika, for Constantin Costa-Gavras's film Amen.**

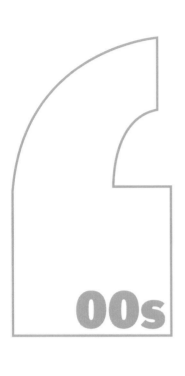

**00s**

One day this giant hook'll appear out of nowhere and yank me back to reality. 'Sorry, Sting, your time's up'
**STING, MUSICIAN**

# STING

## JANUARY 9, 2000

**Sting, 48, left the band the Police in 1984 to go solo. He and his wife, Trudie Styler, have four children; he has two from his first marriage. They live in Tuscany, Wiltshire, London and New York.**

**I'm usually out** of bed by 6.30. My dad was a milkman, so early mornings have never been a problem. First stop is the steam room. I don't like soaps and I don't use shampoo or deodorants. I hate to come out smelling like a product – I actually like my own smell. Then I clean my teeth, wipe my arse and get ready for a few hours of yoga – I can do things with my body at 48 that I couldn't do when I was 20. Breakfast – fresh fruit salad and carrot juice – comes after yoga, otherwise I end up with half-digested food all over the floor. We bought this house in Highgate about 13 years ago. It's got a lot of good memories. I remember taking my son Jake down to the cellar one day and we found all the Police 7in vinyl singles. He wanted to know what these funny round black things were. I told him our entire fortune was based on the sale of these artefacts. He wouldn't believe me.

My housekeeper, Maria, made me some fish for lunch. We have a housekeeper and a butler in Italy, too. Well, it's not like Jeeves and Wooster; he just answers the door. Trudie and I are quite sociable – some nights we might have 30 or 40 for dinner. I never cook, I'm terrible. The last time was about 1974 – baked beans. After lunch, I'll be jumping into a record-company car to go and record the Des O'Connor Show. Then I'll fly straight back to Italy. We've hired a private jet today, but I have been thinking about buying my own plane. With luck, I should be back about 11-ish. If the kids are with us, the first thing I'll do is go and see them while they're asleep. I love doing that. Most nights I'll lie awake wondering, "How did I get to be so lucky?" I'm just worried one of these days this giant hook's going to appear out of nowhere and yank me back to reality. "Sorry, Sting, your time's up." If it did all end tomorrow, as long as I got to keep my family, I'd be happy. Well, perhaps one of the houses, too. And maybe an estate! **In 2001 the Arab-American Institute Foundation gave Sting its Kahlil Gibran Spirit of Humanity Award.**

# TANYA STREETER
## JANUARY 2, 2000

**Tanya Streeter, 26, holds four world freediving records, her deepest to 113 metres. She was formerly social secretary to the governor of Grand Cayman, where she lives with her husband, Paul.**

**Breakfast is Coco** Pops or Frosties. I'll throw on a bikini, and maybe some waterproof mascara. On a record day, I avoid everyone, especially my mother. She gives me lingering "Are you going to be okay?" looks, which grate on me. Paul knows when to get out of the way. He says: "Hey, baby, it's no big deal – you've done it before." Exactly what I want to hear.

From midday it's countdown time. I put on my wetsuit. It gives me some protection from the jellyfish – I once got stung so badly on my face that my lips looked like they'd had surgical implants. We carry cider vinegar for the pain. It beats having someone pee on your face, like we did as kids. If I'm diving for a record, it's important to keep the boat's rope in view – it keeps you going vertically and holds the tag marks to mark the different depths. I kick for the first 15 metres, then my body becomes negatively buoyant and I'll start to freefall. You can't descend quicker than your body allows, because you need to keep equalising the air in

# Your legs are burning from lack of oxygen, you see sunlight above you

your ears. Once I'm at the required depth I won't have breathed for over a minute. The oxygen in my muscles will have been conserved during the freefall, and I'll have just enough for the ascent. I kick like mad until I'm 20 metres from the surface, then I have to slow down. It takes an inordinate amount of control to stop kicking when you've been without air nearly three minutes, your legs are burning from lack of oxygen and you see sunlight above you. I've seen many divers panic. They've got no oxygen left, so the body begins pumping carbon dioxide around the system and they pass out. We call it doing a Samba. They go into spasm, like they're dancing. But blacking out is the body's safety mechanism. Our vocal chords constrict over the trachea and our windpipe closes, which stops us swallowing water and drowning.

It takes all my effort to eat something before I fall into bed. Before I turn the light out I make sure I have a clear airway – no pillows or sheets next to my face. And I can't stand Paul exhaling in my space, so I'll tell him: "Go exhale somewhere else."
**In 2002 Tanya broke both the women's and the men's No-Limits Freediving World records with a 160-metre dive.**

# PHILIP ROSS
## OCTOBER 22, 2000

**Philip Ross, 45, lives at Ravenswood, a village for people with learning difficulties. He is now able to express himself for the first time, by pointing to letters on a keyboard, aided by a carer. It took many hours of work over several months to tell his story.**

**I get woken** by staff at 7am and they chase me so I won't be late for work. I do not care. They are lucky to have me. They love me, so I think: "Give them plenty to do so they don't get bored." I get bored easily so please, be interesting, otherwise I really will go to sleep. On wet days, I won't go out. I am weak with cold and winter. Winter and I will never get along. I hide indoors. Always do dancing to music, in front of the mirror to Elvis, for a jolly long time. He really is the King. Then I go to my classes – weaving, dyeing, felt-making. I get cross if people don't understand me. Voice is gone. Don't know why. I love my room; books by my bed, music very loud. I like all music, classic, rock, ballroom and disco dancing and I love Elvis. He makes me happy. I have a video, given me by my mum. Mum liked Elvis. She died a year ago. She was lovely, we had a good time. She loved to laugh. Jokes. Silly things. I miss my mama a lot but I think she will always be there for me.

I love to paint and I have sold two paintings for £100. Good, eh? When I am sad I use big strokes. When I'm happy, bright colours, smaller marks, more control. I like blood red, stars and silver, rich colours, real arty-smarty. There is a pain in my heart and painting releases my soul.

## Always do dancing to music, in front of the mirror to Elvis, for a jolly long time

Best time of day is yawning in the dusk in my room. The falling sun colours are pretty. Shirley cooks dinner. I love meatballs, chips, spaghetti and naughty apple crumble. I like all the staff, but management gets on my nerves. I sleep on my own. I would like someone to sleep with me. I have a girlfriend, Rachel. Our love is strong. We like to kiss and cuddle but we cannot even have the door closed. It isn't right. I lie in bed and think of what I'll do the next day. I want to go to an Elvis show. But I'm afraid of going on the bus – people are so rude. I dream, of people loving me.
**Philip Ross died in January 2003 of respiratory failure following pneumonia and an asthma attack.**

# DOLLY PARTON

## JUNE 10, 2001

**Dolly Parton was born in Tennessee's Smoky Mountains, the fourth of 12 children, and rose to become a legendary country singer and actress. She lives in Nashville with her husband, Carl Dean.**

**I'm almost always** up by 3am. First thing I do, I go straight to the coffee pot. I've got to get my coffee going. I brush my teeth, brush my hair and just kinda get the morning out of my face. If I have mail or birthday cards to send, I do my paperwork, but I've already put on something to cook. I still cook like the old country women back home – big pots of stuff like chicken and dumpling and roasts and then I'll call my sisters or friends and go: "I've cooked this, do you want to come by and get some?"

My husband will come staggering down. It takes him a few hours to get his head going. I wanna chat and talk and he'll say: "I don't wanna talk. Just be quiet. You've had too much coffee." Of course I have to put on a little make-up because I never know who's going to stop by. And at least if my husband's running in and out of the house, he don't have to look at a tacky woman all day. I love wigs, but I don't usually wear wigs at home because my own hair is blonde and about shoulder-length.

I travel with my junk. I travelled to London for four days with 14 pieces of luggage, but that was also my girlfriend's luggage and the guy that does my hair. But I just can't travel light. I'm serious, I carry everything. My microwave, my coffee pot, my own coffee, my candles, my incense. I don't pack neat either, I just cram it in. I must have my electric blanket, summer or winter. I'm just one of those people that has to feel cosy, even if I have it on low. Right in there now, in my little motel room, my bed's as warm as toast.

If I'm in Nashville, I go to the office a couple of times a week. There's a place called Arnold's that makes soul food. On Thursdays, they have my favourite thing – chicken livers over rice with mashed potatoes, macaroni and pinto beans – so I order all that stuff and bring it up to the apartment next to my office. I can stretch that over two or three days. Just heat it back up in my microwave.

I can honestly say that I enjoy all of my lives. I enjoy the travelling and I'm very close to my family. Some of my sisters are the best friends I have in the whole world. But I think the thing I love the most is my songwriting.

> I can't travel light. I carry everything. My microwave, my coffee pot, my own coffee, my electric blanket

That's my personal time, when I feel closest to God, in a place that I call the "God zone". Not that my songs are all that great, it's just that I feel close to that source, that thing that feeds me and guides me.

In the evenings, nothing's more relaxing to me than to get a great book, get me a big jug of Kool-Aid or Coke, curl up under my electric blanket with a bunch of pillows and just read and read. I couldn't be lazy-minded. I'll never retire. I hope to die doing something I'm loving, right on stage, in the middle of a song. **Dolly Parton released a new album, Halos and Horns, in 2002. She has now been signed up to star as Mae West in a movie.**

# CHRISTOPHER REEVE
## APRIL 14, 2002

**The actor Christopher Reeve, 49, was paralysed from the neck down in a showjumping accident in 1995. He runs the Christopher Reeve Paralysis Foundation from his home in upstate New York, where he lives with his wife, Dana, and son Will, 9.**

**I'm never disabled** in my dreams. I'll be sailing, riding, making films. I wake up about 6.30, feeling more like stone than flesh because I've lain rigid all night. At about 7.30 the nurse and an aide come in and we do exercises which help turn me back into flesh and blood. And I have to be washed and dressed. I have a gym and three times a week I'm lifted onto a special bike, my feet are strapped onto the pedals, electrodes stimulate the muscles – and I can ride a bike! Then I go into my office. Over the last five years I've flown to almost every state. I speak at schools, rehab centres, success seminars, meetings of neuroscientists... Much of my day is spent on the phone or giving dictation. I work through lunch. The emphasis is on protein, and to avoid foods that create gas. I work till about 4pm, then Will comes home and I get him set up with his homework. Often he joins me in the office. He plays on a hockey team, so we'll go out and he'll shoot against the goal we have in the driveway and I'll coach. Then comes the most difficult part of my day: for at least an hour I take the hose off. In 1995 I could only

## I'm never disabled in my dreams. I'll be sailing, riding, making films...

breathe unaided for 90 seconds. I'd have to pull with my neck and shoulders. Now I have the strength to breathe using my diaphragm. Dana and I have a rule: you never talk about medical issues at the dinner table. Three times a week we'll go to the movies, visit friends. I have a nurse with me, because the ventilator can fail at any moment. We carry an ambu-bag – like a balloon with an attachment. Someone squeezes it to get air into my lungs while they figure out what's wrong. Usually a piece of hose has come loose. I don't really stress out about it any more.

I go to bed at 9.30 because it takes two hours. There's a nurse downstairs listening to my breathing on a monitor during the night, but there are certain times when we turn the monitor off so Dana and I can have our own time together.
**In 2003 Reeve became the third patient in medical history to have electrodes implanted in his diaphragm to stimulate regular breathing. He has also regained his sense of smell.**

**Johnny Vegas, aka Michael Pennington, 32, comedian and entertainer, stars in the TV drama Happiness. He and his wife, Catherine, an interior designer, 27, have homes in St Helens, Merseyside, and London.**

**The first thing** I do when I wake up is have a fag. I'm trying to give them up, but it's still 30 a day – at least. Things have improved, though… when I was on Benson & Hedges, I'd be coughing my lungs out for a good 15 minutes before I could light up my first one, but since switching to Marlboro Lights, the smoker's cough's gone, so I haven't got that 15-minute hold-up any more. I'm not saying that as any kind of endorsement – it's just one of life's small bonuses.

I bought this house in St Helens three years ago. It's got six bedrooms, which seems excessive for just the two of us, I know, but I paid a lot less for it than you would for a shed in South Kensington. The guy who had it before us did loads of DIY, but he got nothing right. He put a serving hatch in one of the bedrooms, for God's sake! Even the flock wallpaper was upside down. At one point, I thought I'd bought the Alton Towers of the building trade. And I come from a building family, so I know a thing or two. My dad and a brother are both joiners. I guess I could've become a joiner, but my life changed completely when I discovered pottery at school. I could sit with a slab of clay for hours – I ended up doing a degree in ceramics. One of my proudest moments was creating two jugs in the shape of a pair of Bermuda shorts – beauty and practicality merged into one. But then I tried my luck at stand-up instead and that just took off.

If I'm in St Helens, I might pop round to Mum's. Funny thing is, I've noticed lately that what I'll do is say hello and then automatically go straight to the fridge, even if I don't want anything. It's like Tony in The Sopranos; I'll take out the cheese and put it back in again just as a way of contributing to family life. Actually, Dad's often got a pot of his homemade broth on the go. He uses a ham shank and lentils – a recipe his mum taught him. It's a life-saver, literally. He used to take it in to this old lady living on our street who said it was the only thing keeping her going. But her family must have hated Dad because they were trying to get her into a home and were like: "We want to sell the bloody house – stop interfering." Mum and Dad are my heroes, whatever the neighbours think. And now being married to Catherine is just the best thing. In fact, I knew she was the one the day I met her. Sure, there's going to be rows and tantrums, but whatever comes along, we'll work it out. And if that means watching another night of her favourite reality-TV programmes then it's worth it. Then, of course, there's our different taste in music. She's up on everything and thinks I've got terrible tastes. But when I'm out, I know she plays my Sinatra records. Unlike me, she's vegetarian, but that's fine, she's a great cook. We get invited to loads of

## Admittedly there were times that I'd feel: 'God, if only I could get back onto solids'

parties, but to be honest we're very homely and don't bother with a lot of them. I know this might seem odd, considering I've got such a reputation for going out and getting drunk, but it's true. Admittedly, I've got the capacity to drink right through to the next morning and right through the next day, but where I come from I'd never be considered a big boozer – though there were times I'd feel: "God, if only I could get back onto solids."

I'm quite an insomniac, but luckily I can do really well on three hours' sleep. If I can't get to sleep, I just get up and use the time for reading or writing. It's great – there aren't all those daytime distractions like the phone, the telly… the serving hatch. And it's not like I can start a wash or get the Hoover out. I suppose I could polish the surfaces.

Up to now, everything I've been involved in has been a laugh. The main thing is I haven't sh** on anyone to get where I am, and if it all went down the pan tomorrow, I wouldn't suddenly be a failure. Somebody said to my dad once that he must be really proud of me now I'm famous, and my dad just answered back: "I always was." At the end of the day that alone is enough for me. Everything else is a bonus.

**In January 2003 Johnny Vegas accused Viz magazine of reneging on their promise to pay him £1 for his wedding photographs.**

# ZOYA
## AUGUST 5, 2001

**Zoya, 23, is an active member of the Revolutionary Afghan Women's Association. She teaches and campaigns clandestinely throughout Afghanistan, which is ruled by the hardline Taliban regime.**

**I usually get** up at sunrise because the people we visit live without electricity. Like all Afghan women I have to put on the burqa, the shroud. I hide my leaflets under it. The Taliban say schools are a gateway to hell, the first step towards prostitution. They are a bunch of illiterate criminals. Under Taliban rules, women can't even go shopping on their own – they'll take their five-year-old son, anyone they can find. And they can't be seen or touched by male doctors. But for the Taliban it's better to let their own wives die and guarantee them paradise.

I never use my real name, and I don't know the real names of the people I work with. But I've come to realise danger is everywhere and I no longer feel the fear. I'm ready to sacrifice myself if I have to. I haven't had a private life for years. I haven't got the time even to talk about whether I want to fall in love. I could join my relatives in the States, but I would be ashamed to accept an American lifestyle. To me it would be a form of treason. My relatives don't even admit to having Afghan origins. They have

hearts as small as those of birds. What keeps me going is what I see. There's a stadium in Kabul where people get lashed or stoned, or have their hands cut off, or are executed. It's announced the day before on the radio, and everyone is encouraged to watch. Once I went there. It was the day they were cutting hands off. I saw lots of children and teenagers in the stands. They were laughing their heads off. I try to imagine their future. They will all become criminals if we go on like this.

**Following this piece, Zoya's Story: An Afghan Woman's Battle for Freedom was published in 16 countries. She is now working in an Afghan refugee camp in Pakistan.**

# Danger is everywhere but I no longer feel fear. I'm ready to sacrifice myself

# GORDON RAMSAY

## JANUARY 14, 2001

**The chef Gordon Ramsay, 34, recently voted Chef of the Year, now runs his eponymous restaurant in Chelsea. He lives in Battersea with his wife, Tana, their daughter Megan, 2, and twins, Jack and Holly, 1.**

**I remember walking** into the kitchen one morning, absolutely shattered. My eyes were stuck together. The chef said: "How long did you sleep last night?" I said: "About five and a half hours." He said: "Too long." This was in Paris – I actually thought he said "Toulon", like the sausage. But he went on to say that by the time I was 60 I'd have wasted 20 years of my life. I've slept less since then. Tana brings up tea and toast before 7am. I eat it quickly – if I don't Megan insists on smearing it on my head. Tana burns toast. I dedicated A Chef For All Seasons to Megan, Jack and Holly, hoping they follow in their father's footsteps, not their mother's. She's gradually getting better. I think what holds her back is cooking for infants. There's no salt. It's all puree. And 90% of it ends up on the floor. People say, "Why do you never feed the twins?" If I was a traffic warden, maybe I would. But I'm a cook; I'm not interested in seeing my food go everywhere.

I'm at work by 8am on the dot. The night cook's already dipped all the chocolates, made all the bread, and piped all the macaroons. First thing is a cup of tea. When you're running something as fine as this restaurant, you'd be surprised how basic you want it. So I want PG Tips. Between 12pm and 3pm, it's controlled madness. It's Air Traffic Control. Somebody phoned up once and said: "I'm bringing my 15-year-old son to the restaurant. Will Gordon do him an omelette?" I just went: "Tell him to

f*** off." Will I do him an omelette? If he wants an omelette, try McDonald's. These calls come in the middle of service. You're in a frantic situation and timing is of the essence. You've got six guests at table and their main courses need to be served at the same time. One spanner in the works, and the whole lot goes in the bin.

We have our main meal in the kitchen at 5.30pm. The new cooks in the brigade will cook that. I always ask them to do a pudding – something simple like a leftover-fruit crumble. But for all 38 people in the kitchen. Just so they don't get blasé with the expensive stuff like sea bass, foie gras and truffles. It's been well documented that I need to spend more time in management training school. But I'm running a kitchen here, not some wuss-hole for has-beens that want to appear on Ready Steady Cook.

At 6pm it's ravioli time. It needs to be made fresh twice a day. The chefs then have a meeting to discuss the specials

## Will I do him an omelette? Tell him to f*** off. If he wants an omelette, try McDonald's

and any customer requirements – like any nut-risotto fruitcake vegetarians. And at 7pm, the curtain goes up – bang! There's only one winner. It's like boxing. You can't afford a mediocre bout. I'm sick of the label "celebrity chef" – 99% of them don't even have restaurants. All they worry about is when they're next appearing on Ready Steady Cook. The last pudding goes out around midnight. I leave at 1am and go for a run. At home I get a glass of milk and watch Sky News until I'm tired. I sleep in my pants because I'm fed up of Megan jumping on the bed and playing ding-ding-daddy with my willie. To be honest, I'm looking forward to a weekend away from her. For the first time in ages Tana and I'll be able to sleep without our pants on. **In 2003, Gordon Ramsay's is the only London restaurant with three Michelin stars.**

125

# SOPHIA INGIBIRE TUYISENGE
## APRIL 6, 2003

**Sophia Ingibire Tuyisenge, 12, and her sisters, Claudette, 11, and Solange, 3, live near Kigali in Rwanda. Their father was killed in the genocide in 1994; their mother died two years ago from Aids.**

**My sisters and** I sleep in the same bed since our mother died. Our house has two rooms. I keep our food in old rice sacks and our clean clothes in plastic bags hanging above the floor so they don't get wet when the rain comes in through the hole in the tin roof. First I light a paraffin lamp. Then I climb down the hill with jerrycans to get water from the pump. They are heavy, and when it is raining the ground gets muddy, so you can slip. We make porridge, which we eat out of plastic mugs.

When Claudette goes to school I wash the mugs, then sweep and scrub the floor. Of course Solange has to help. She copies me, shouting and laughing and brushing away. She can be quite a handful, and sometimes I wish she would stop chattering. But she is our little sister and we love her very much. Really I am her mother now. Our mother began to get sick after she gave birth to Solange. For a long time we looked after her. Then, when she died, our father's family wanted to sell our house, but we did not want to be separated from Solange, so we said we would look after her ourselves. Claudette and I take turns to go to school, one in the morning, the other in the afternoon, so we can look after Solange. I give her a bath. I take the basin outside, pour in the water, and she jumps in. I wash her hair and give her ears and her nails a good

# I miss my mother so much. She said we should be brave and God would look after us

scrub while she splashes around. I dry her and rub Vaseline into her skin, like my mother showed me. I cook rice with cassava for our main meal. Sometimes I go to the petrol station and buy two litres of paraffin. I pour it into empty Fanta bottles to sell at the bottom of the path to our house. It pays for soap and vegetables. I think about my mother as I lie in bed. I miss her so much. She said we should be brave and have no fear because God would look after us. We can see that is true: we are coping just fine. **Sophia and her sisters are waiting for a house in a children's village supported by the Survivors Fund.**

127

# BARBARA WINDSOR

## MAY 6, 2001

**Barbara Windsor, 63, famed for her Carry On roles, plays Peggy Mitchell in EastEnders. She received an MBE in 1999 and last year married Scott Mitchell, 38, a recruitment consultant. They live in London.**

**During the week** I get up about quarter to six. There are three things I must take in the morning. My three puffs, because I'm asthmatic. Then my HRT. The doctor said it would be good for my complexion and make me feel great, but I always tend to feel great, so I don't really know what effect it's having. And then an aspirin. I had a mini-stroke about seven years ago, just after I had my hysterectomy. At the time, I was in my 50s and running around the stage, doing two shows a day as Aladdin. I hadn't relaxed in ages. I learnt my lesson.

I have a bath rather than a shower, because I don't like water running over my face. And I've always had very fine hair that turns to nothing if it gets wet. That's why I've relied on wigs over the years. Then I'll go and get the papers – all the tabloids and one heavyweight.

At the BBC, I have my own dressing room with a TV, a radio and a put-you-up. I ring Scott to let him know I'm in okay and then the girls do my make-up and wardrobe fittings. You've got to be careful about continuity. The only time I goofed, one of the crew ran onto the set saying: "You've got the wrong colour nail varnish on, Bar!" Viewers notice things like that.

We've got our own canteen. If I'm good, it's toast or fruit salad, but there's nothing like the smell of sausages and bacon wafting down the corridor, so I usually grab a sausage before going on set. Off set, I just wear something like a pair of casual trousers. I don't like things that crease. And I like clothes to match. I can't have blue here and black there. My mother always said I had to be co-ordinated. She was a wonderful dressmaker, who worked in the West End – which women from the East End didn't really do in those days. Because of my height and big bosoms she'd say: "No stripes going across, no polka dots." I think it broke her heart I didn't turn out slim, tall, dark-haired, with a plum in my mouth – she even sent me to elocution lessons. She always wanted me to better myself.

When things have been bad in my life, I've always taken great solace in being able to go on stage and say to an audience: "'Allo, everyone, here I am!" I went on the night I buried Mummy. I really bottled up all the grief I had. It was years later before it all poured out. Then, when my first husband, Ronnie [Knight], was up for murder and arson, I was doing pantomime and people said: "How can you get out there?" But getting a shot in the arm of the public's warmth became like a medicine to me.

Lunch is usually at 1.30. I often go to the canteen with June Brown, who's Dot in EastEnders. Then I might go into the green room for a gossip, or maybe someone will have had a drama the night before, so you'll try to help them sort it out. I get called "little mother courage".

## Once they asked me to appear on Question Time. I said: 'Are you mental?'

My first taste of performing was during the war, when I was evacuated to Blackpool and started dance classes. Then when I came home I won a scholarship to a girls' Catholic school. I wanted to become a nun then – Mummy would catch me walking around the kitchen with a tea towel over my head saying Hail Marys. I was 15 when I got my first role in the West End. Actually, people always think of me as this great Carry On figure, but really I've had more of a topsy-turvy life of matinées, evening performances and being on tour. Now, with EastEnders it's wonderful – I'm a nine-to-five person.

Scott's a wonderful husband. I'm very contented – so contented I've actually stuck on 7lb. On a little girl like me that's a hell of a lot. I love Question Time. I sit there ranting at what they're all saying. Once they asked me to appear on the show, and I said: "Are you mental?" Before bed, I take my make-up off, and maybe do a bit of reading or rabbiting to Scott – unless we've been out and I've had one cocktail too many. Before I turn out the light, I say one Our Father and three Hail Marys. It makes me think that everything's going to be okay. **Barbara took extended leave from EastEnders early in 2003, suffering from the Epstein-Barr virus, a strain of glandular fever. She hopes to return to the soap in 2004.**

# ALICE COOPER

## SEPTEMBER 16, 2001

**The singer Alice Cooper, 53, recently released his 28th album, Dragontown. He lives in Paradise Valley, Arizona, with his wife, Sheryl, and their three children, Dashiell, Sonora and Calico.**

**Here are Alice** Cooper's grooming secrets. I tie back my hair and put on some shades. Well, when you wake up in the morning and see perfection staring back at you, there's not much you can improve upon. Then I eat a huge breakfast. I have a strict non-vegetarian diet. I love those hotel buffet breakfasts – sausages, bacon, eggs. The reason I can eat so much is because I burn off so many calories. I walk incessantly. It doesn't matter where I am – at home, in London, Moscow, New York City – I can easily cover 10 or 20 miles a day. Flea markets, that's where you'll find me. I'm always picking up the dumbest things. The last time I went on tour, I went away with two suitcases and I went back home with 14.

In the 70s, instead of walking from shop to shop, I used to walk from bar to bar. I drank all day and every day. I was doing five shows a week in front of 15,000 people for two whole years. I was a complete wreck. Every night I'd drink a little more, just to help me get by. Basically, I have to be on a hospital bed before I can say "Stop". And that's what happened. My wife put me in a limo and sent me to an insane asylum. When I came out a month later I was dry. Now I've quit, I have to find something else to fill all that time I used to spend in the bar. That's why I walk, that's why I shop, and that's why I play golf. I hate down time. I get bored very easily. And then I get depressed.

Come lunchtime, I'll usually eat something very light, like sushi. I never cook. God, that's a frightful thought! I can barbecue and that's about my level. At home I go out on the ranch, rope myself a steer, slap it on the grill and eat it. Home is a place called Paradise Valley, which I always think sounds like a funeral home. All the kids live at home at the moment. I think I'm a pretty good dad. At least my kids can never say: "Dad, you don't understand how we feel." I must be the only father that bangs on the bedroom door and says: "Turn that music up!"

The birth of my first daughter coincided with the time that I started thinking about Christianity. I do come from a Christian background. My father was a pastor. These days, I rock harder than I've ever rocked. If I write a song

I think I'm a pretty good dad. I must be the only one who bangs on the bedroom door saying: 'Turn that music up!'

about horror, I'm actually writing about real horror – eternal damnation. I find the real world a very shocking place. Some of the stuff that happens today is not that far removed from what happened in Nazi Germany. Look at the genocides in Albania, Bosnia, Africa. That's horror. People think it's ironic that this evil Alice Cooper character – this rock'n'roll rebel – is a Christian. But, to me, being a Christian is the most rebellious thing I've ever done in my life. Drinking beer is easy. Trashing your hotel room is easy. But being a Christian, that's a tough call. That's real rebellion.

**Alice Cooper is touring and working on his next album, which is due for release in early 2004.**

# BERYL COOK
## DECEMBER 2, 2001

**Beryl Cook OBE, 75, was formerly a showgirl and a model and ran a boarding house. She has been painting for 40 years. She lives in Bristol. Her husband and son are both named John.**

**Norma Major told** me that a Teasmaid is very naff. I realised immediately that I was naff and very happy to be so. I go straight to my painting room. I absolutely love painting. I think people like my pictures because they're ordinary, like themselves, and like me. People say I'm the most popular artist in England – I don't take a blind bit of notice. I only paint to please myself. I paint women like me, but I'm not really like them at all. I'm shy and nervous. I wish I had the temperament of the ladies in my paintings so I could do the things they do: tap-dancing, singing. I seem so jolly and I laugh a lot. Actually, that's my cover.

I bring a Thermos to my painting room and I listen to Radio 4, but I think Woman's Hour is awful now with all this feminism. At 4.30 I watch Countdown and tick off what I'm going to watch that night, if we're not going out. I absolutely love television. But after 35 years I've given up Coronation Street, which has lost all its charm and humour. It's trying to get more like EastEnders and bringing in these dreadful youngsters. If we're staying in, John'll cook. I'm terribly common. I like shepherd's pie; corned-beef hash. I hate going out to dinner and I can't eat fussy food.

# Women of a certain class have more spunk... my class, working class

When we first came to Bristol we had a lot of invitations and poor John had to fend everyone off and make excuses: "Beryl's not very well, or Beryl's got a whitlow on her finger." I once had a real whitlow and I put a bread poultice on it, but when I took it off the Siamese cat came and ate it. Fame and success have made me feel entitled to be honest and refuse to do anything I don't want to. We go to jazz pubs twice or even three times a week. I watch the women and I think: "Jolly good luck to you!" They're determined to dress up, go out and have a good time. Women of a certain class have more spunk. My class – working class. Sitting in the pub I'll do little drawings of people in my notebook in my handbag. Let's face it, I'm a voyeur. By 10.30 we're absolutely buggered and we go home to bed.
**Beryl Cook's irrepressible characters will be coming to life in Bosom Pals, a pair of animated films, with the voices of Dawn French, Alison Steadman and Timothy Spall.**

# KIMBERLEY BAILEY

## MARCH 24, 2002

**Kimberley Bailey, 15, who has multiple disabilities, has won 13 national gold medals for swimming. She is the youngest of six children and lives with her mother, Christine Bailey, in West Sussex.**

**I can't go** anywhere until I've got my leg on, so I have my clothes on a chair next to my bed. I'm used to the leg – I've been wearing one since the real one was amputated when I was three. Mum says when God was giving out body parts, he got mine a bit scrambled. I was born without an anus and so many other problems, the list was a mile long. No one thought I'd survive. I had curvature of the spine, a webbed neck, dislocated hips. My ribs were fused, I had a wasted left leg, my thumbs were like fingers, I had club feet, a cleft palate… What a nightmare! I was doubly incontinent until I was seven, and the doctor said there was nothing they could do. Finally I couldn't stand nappies any longer and trained myself to use the toilet.

At school, my friends Melissa, Michelle and Daniella are waiting. The day I got my new chair, everyone was fighting over who'd push it: "Let me! No, let me!" And I went: "Actually, *I'm* going to push it…" Some teachers treat me softer because I've got problems. I hate that. It was a fantastic moment when I was picked for the

## Mum says when God was giving out the body parts he got mine a bit scrambled

England squad a year ago. Four evenings a week I train at the Aquarena in Worthing. Mum comes to help me change. I do feel a bit sorry for her. Dad left when I was a baby, and it's difficult financially. She saves a bit here and there on the shopping, or holds a boot sale. Now a local charity called Miracles has offered to help fundraise, which felt like a miracle in itself. We're trying to raise £10,000 before the Paralympics in 2004.

It takes ages to get ready for bed. Sometimes I have a bit of a stomp and ask: "Why me? Why am I like this?" But at the end of the day, okay, life can be a struggle, but it's also a gift and it's up to me to make the best of it.

**Owing to the lack of a suitable one-to-one coach in her area, Kimberley had to abandon her plans for the 2004 Paralympics. She is now setting her sights on Beijing in 2008 and is studying for her A-levels.**

# NELSON MANDELA
## OCTOBER 13, 2002

**Nelson Mandela, 84, who spent 27 years in prison for treason, was South Africa's president from 1994 to 1999. He lives in Johannesburg. His third wife is the worldwide literacy campaigner, Graca Machel.**

**I wake at** 4.30 every morning. After over two decades of the same routine in prison it is difficult to change. I left my village in April 1941, but it has not left me, so I take a simple breakfast – just two spoons of porridge with nuts and hot milk. Then slices of kiwi fruit and banana. I used to be very particular about my clothes. But now I don't like to tie myself up with ties and waistcoats. Sometimes I argue with my wife when there are state occasions. She says: "Please put on a suit, you can't go out like that." And I say to her: "What would you say to the president of Nigeria, then?" I think I have won the argument now.

I am a stickler for punctuality – not only because it's a sign of respect to the person you are meeting, but in order to combat the Western stereotype of Africans being late. I always break for lunch. I like vegetables very much, and salad. And beans. I do drink wine, although I'm a bit uncultivated as I can only drink sweet wine. I try resting

after lunch. In jail they thought we were so dangerous they watched us even when we slept. So we got used to napping under any conditions. I have felt fear more times than I can remember, but I hide it behind a mask of boldness. If you are miserable, you will have horror stories in your dreams. But I am always positive.

**Mandela has now been awarded honorary degrees from more than 50 international universities.**

# FRODO
## NOVEMBER 12, 2000

**Frodo, 3, is trained to perform domestic tasks for his disabled owner. He lives in Southend with Stephanie Pengelly, 47, who has familial spastic paraplegia; her three children are also affected.**

**I've got a** rug on the floor but I like to wake up on the bed next to Steph. It's a comfort thing. She's pretty ropey in the morning, to be honest, whereas I'm totally chipper. Just can't wait to get up and get going. As soon as the alarm goes off I roll over and lick her face to wake her up. Then I get the rubber tug toy and pull her up to a sitting position. We have a little bit of chitchat: "Morning, Frodo, how are you today?" Bit of a cuddle. Then a root about under the bed to find her slippers and her elbow crutches, drag them out with a minimum of slobber – no excuse for that – and we're away.

Once Steph's up, I follow her everywhere. I tug the bathroom light on and lurk around purposefully in case she drops something. The truth is, just between you and me, she's not completely safe without me. I'm so tuned into her, I can hear a crutch fall across a ploughed field, and in two secs I'll be

# VINNIE JONES

## JANUARY 13, 2002

**Vinnie Jones, 37, played football for several clubs including Wimbledon and Leeds, but is now a full-time film actor. He lives in Hertfordshire with his wife, Tanya, and 14-year-old stepdaughter, Kaley.**

**I don't sleep** that well. There's too much going off in my head. Cos I'm, like, this big thinker, y'know. I've never done breakfast. Just a cup of tea and the Racing Post. I shower, shave, brush my teeth, do me hair, moisturise my face and I'm ready. I got into moisturisers when I played football. I always wanted to be famous. The big house and big car were the only things that seemed important. I wanted to follow in my dad's footsteps. Funny thing is, these days he has a go at me. He says: "Here comes the film star. Goes to work for an hour and earns a million quid." I really get the hump with him. He can be a prat at times.

Sometimes I spend the afternoon at the gym. I love it when mates come up and say: "Cor blimey, you're looking well, son." I've still got a good set of ab-doms, the six-pack and all that. I work hard at anything I do. When I went to Hollywood, I thought I was Robert-f***ing-De-Niro. I

## I've got a seriously low tolerance level to people who want to have a go at me

didn't give a sh** about anyone. A lot of people see me as this very angry man. Maybe it's because I'm competitive. If people start taking the mick, that gets my goat. I've got a seriously low tolerance level to people who want to have a go at me. Tanz is the one who keeps me together when I do really lose it with people. If I really f*** up big time, she's the one who'll see me break down and cry.

Last night I was out lamping with my dad till 2. We saw eight foxes in a mile radius. If Tanz is awake when I get in, we'll have a chat, and I kiss Kaley goodnight. I slept better when I played football. If I had one bad game, no one noticed. But if I have one bad film, everybody notices. If anyone has a go at my acting, that really slaughters me. I get nightmares about bad reviews. One or two people have tried to put the boot in. They know who they are. More importantly, I know who they are.

**Vinnie is soon to appear in The Big Bounce, with Morgan Freeman. His blues and soul album, released in 2002 and entitled Respect, was not a hit.**

there. It wasn't always like this. Ooh no, no. To begin with it was dire. A personality clash, you could say. She was, "Frodo, do this," "Frodo, do that," and I'm like: "Sorry. What did your last slave die of?" Washing it was, mostly. What is this thing with humans and washing? She expected me to drag great baskets of it out of the machine and into the garden. And then she'd freak when it all spilt out and got a bit muddy. But Steph's a forgiving little thing, and we love each other dearly now. Once I've helped her get dressed, passing her this and that, it's off to the bank – I grab the money from the cashpoint – then I take her prescription into the chemist and hand that over. My favourite is ASDA. I get all we need off the shelves, very gently, always monitoring the slobber thing. Then, at the checkout, my pièce de résistance: handing over the purse. The queue behind us will be in raptures. So easily amused, humans.

At night, I stand guard while the carer bathes her, then I help her into bed and settle down beside her. She needs me close. Especially if she's not well.

**Since being interviewed, Frodo has won three awards, including The Golden Bone Award for Devotion to Duty.**

# PHAN THI KIM PHUC

**Phan Thi Kim Phuc was 9 when Nick Ut's photograph of Vietnamese napalm victims made her an icon. Kim, 37, now a Unesco goodwill ambassador, lives near Toronto.**

**Sometimes we have** noodle soup for breakfast, but my children love all things Canadian, so they have cereal and pancakes. But they also know how to be Vietnamese. My mom makes sure they use their chopsticks. They know their mommy suffered. Thomas, my little boy, looked at the skin on my arms one day when he was just a baby, and he could see the difference. He kissed me and he said: "That hurts, Mommy?" He knew something bad had happened. As a teenager I thought I'd never have children. Who would want me with my burnt skin? But my husband is such a lovely man. Every day I thank God for giving me my husband and my children and for setting me free. Escaping Vietnam was hard. When we jumped plane in 1992 we had refugee status, we had no money and no place to live. But Canada is our home now.

Before the war, we lived in a big house in Trang Bang. We had a farm, and me and my brothers wanted for nothing. I remember the war coming to my village. It was the summertime of 1972, and my mom decided to go to the temple – we thought nothing bad would happen in a holy place. Just as we finished our lunch, we heard the noise of the aeroplanes. I saw four bombs raining down. I didn't hear the big explosion – just *boop, boop, boop, boop,* and then fire all over my body and my clothes burning off. I was so scared, so scared. Just crying and running and crying, running until I couldn't run any more. When I stopped, one of the soldiers gave me water. He tried to pour it on my back but I screamed: "*Nong qua, nong qua!*" "Too hot, too hot!" Napalm burns at 800 ° to 1200 °C, and it sticks. Nothing can stop it – it burns through flesh and muscle and internal organs until it is finished. Every day the nurses cut off the dead flesh, and the pain was terrible, horrible. But I wanted to live so bad. When I came home, after 14 months, my parents showed me the picture. And I thanked God for my feet. Because if not for my feet I would have died in that fire – and then who would know?

I set up the Kim Foundation for child victims of war. I have no money, but I have my story and I have compassion and I believe telling the world about the horror of war is

## I saw four bombs rain down. Then fire all over my body and my clothes burning off

# MR PEARL
## MARCH 4, 2001

**'Mr Pearl', 39, a South African ex-ballet dancer, makes corsets for Vivienne Westwood, Christian Lacroix and Dior and many wealthy private clients. His own waist is 18in. He lives in London and Paris**

**Some days one** wakes up very nervous. Being a pessimist is not always a pleasure. First I choose a corset for the day. It is like my armour. Psychologically and physically, it is comforting. It makes me feel part of the insect world. I am fascinated by wasps and bees because their waists are so extraordinary. I take a quick bath, no frills, and powder my body with baby powder and then wrap around a sheath of silk, which lies between the corset and one's skin. I normally have three on the go. They are kept rolled up in the cupboard and aired from time to time. I am not interested in the smoothers and minimisers of today's fashion – garments which have that dreadful word "stretch".

I have a Paris atelier. Designers there have more empathy with corsetry. We start at 10am and my workshop turns into a human hive. There are mountains of cotton, raw silk, beads, steel, metal cutters and an eyelet machine. The most challenging aspect of my work is the fitting of each corset. I have to work on skin and flesh, because the body is malleable. A mannequin is not. Sometimes nine fittings are required and each can take two hours. It exhausts me. One of my favourite clients is Jerry Hall.

## I live in a sort of cocoon. I have joined the insect world. I have my own shell

She is very, very charming and has an exquisite waist. My own goal is to squeeze into a 16in corset. Unfortunately I have bones which I cannot change unless I am operated on. Bones are like walls – they frustrate me. My ideal is a different waist, more tapered. It's a work in progress. I cannot be without a corset. I would just feel wrong. It can make you light-headed and often I have fainted. The oxygen doesn't flow as freely, and I believe it changes the way the brain functions. Doctors are horrified. But it almost heightens the experience of having a brain.

After a hard day I don't want to see anybody. I sleep in a corset or a very thick belt, and sleep comes gracefully. I live in a sort of cocoon. I have joined the insect world. I have my own shell. Why should I wish to leave that?
**Mr Pearl has broadened his horizons (though not his waistline) and has designed the costumes for a ballet, Silent Rhythms, by the choreographer Matthew Hawkins.**

the right thing to do. When Unesco asked me to be goodwill ambassador, I said: "How can I do this? I am just a mother." They said: "After this terrible thing, you are at peace with yourself. It's enough just to be who you are."

Often we're in bed by 9. I have nightmares if I've seen something on TV about war. Violence upsets me. I try not to see it or let my boys see it. In those dreams I am always a child again, and I'm running, running. I wake up terrified. But then I look round our bedroom and I tell myself: "It's okay. This is my life now. The fear is over."
**Phan Thi Kim Phuc was awarded the Queen's Golden Jubilee medal in 2002. Her foundation is now working to help children in Iraq.**

# MARC BARRY

## OCTOBER 6, 2002

**Marc Barry is a corporate spy. Aged 36, he has his own company, C3I Analytics, based in New York City. He co-wrote Spooked: Espionage in Corporate America. He lives alone in a New York loft apartment.**

**To kick-start** my day I have to drink an obscene amount of coffee around 6.30am. I can barely get from my bed to the kitchen to pour the caffeine down my face. I'm *not* the average person, so I try not to look one. Usually I wear Italian snakeskin boots that rock and have a zip up the side, Selectica 92 sunglasses and a Gucci vintage shirt. I live in a loft with only vintage furniture – everything dates from 1965 to 1972. There's something definitely sexy about a tongue-shaped chair. If it's possible to be sexually attracted to a piece of furniture, then this is it. And my circular bed with the white shag is fantastic. I don't bother telling women any more what I do, because they don't believe me. They think I'm making it up to get them into bed.

Business is warfare. It's that simple. When it comes to legality, I can go right up to the line. I can dance on the line. I just can't *cross* the line, because on the other side is the FBI. I provide companies with actionable intelligence they can't get themselves or don't want to be caught getting. If *I* get caught, well, that's on me. That's why they pay big money. I can earn $2,000 a day, so I net $25,000 for a job, and I work maybe 30 or 40 capers in a year. I'm paid to collect intelligence about a company's marketing plan, or I'll get copies of a rival's business plans. An example: Kraft Foods was about to market a rising-crust pizza, and a competitor wanted all the data he could get. He hired me to target their pizza production line.

I specialise in humint – human intelligence. I target executives. I go after people who have the answer and I get them to see things my way. How? By being a prince of a guy. If he's a golfer, then I'm a golfer. He likes bowling? Then so do I. My clients are usually uptight executives. I'll meet them in restaurants or at my loft to hand over information. It's too dangerous any other way; hackers are everywhere. The Achilles heel for corporations is disgruntled employees. I find them on internet databases where people have posted their resumés. Before I go after somebody, I'll know everything about him. I need to know what buttons to push. I can profile someone within 30 seconds of meeting them. I used to create the same scenarios to meet women. I'd see a woman get into her car

and take the licence plate. Then I'd back up the number to her home, run her credit report, phone bill, see the restaurants she frequented. Unfortunately I wouldn't stop there. But when you start running people's credit reports you get this sanitised version of who that person is, and what you wind up doing is robbing yourself of all the kind of magical things that can happen when you first meet someone. I don't trust anybody. Everyone has a price. It's quite clear-cut: I'm either working for you or against

# I don't tell women what I do. They think I'm making it up to get them into bed

you. Some people are so f★★★ing stupid. If we were baboons or dogs, we'd bite their faces off. I have no illusions of what people are capable of doing to each other. That's why I keep everyone at arm's length until they prove they're worthy of my trust. That includes my family. *Everyone.* Every now and again I'll meet someone who won't give up information, and although it's frustrating I think it's sweet. It means there's hope.

In the evening I go to the gym, hit the weights and run four miles. It keeps the mind sharp. Oh, who am I kidding? It's plumage to get laid. At night I meet friends at one of the clubs in the East Village. Punk clubs, dance clubs, rave places. The kids are all high on ecstasy. I don't drink, I don't do drugs, I don't smoke. Soda water and cranberry is my drink. If I'm running a caper in Europe, I may go to bed at midnight, then get up at 4am and make phone calls. Otherwise I'll just sit back and weird out on my furniture for a while and listen to the BBC broadcast. Then I'll go to bed. I sleep so well, it's beautiful.

**Barry is now a corporate counter-terrorism consultant. After his Life in the Day appeared he was approached by 15 film companies, and a movie telling his story is in development. The part of Barry is to be offered to Brad Pitt.**

# BARRY WHITE
## APRIL 1, 2001

**The soul singer Barry White, aka the Walrus of Love, 56, has eight children from two marriages and lives in San Diego with his partner, Katherine.**

**I get up** about 10 and have Rice Krispies or Raisin Bran, then maybe orange juice, maybe eggs, bacon… I only wear silk pyjamas, which I like to lounge around in during the day – I've got black ones, brown ones, green ones, different colours. Then I like to mess around in my studio, or with my computer games. One of the things I love about making music is you've got a lot of free time. That means I can relax, take it easy. I love to sit and think. In one of the rooms in my house, I have a large salt-water aquarium full of fish from the ocean. About 200 of them. Watching them is very therapeutic. I've always been into nature. My bad habit's the cigarettes. I smoke Benson & Hedges, Ultra Light Menthol. I enjoy them far too much.

I didn't get a proper education, so I didn't graduate from high school. The only thing I really loved was music. My mother taught piano and people would come round to

## They say I'm the King of Love but at the end of the day I'm just king of my own life

our house for their lessons. I would sit in and just listen. I wasn't interested in the scales and all that stuff, but I learnt a lot of things, about music, about people, too. That's the best way to deal with music. It's a feeling. No one said you need to read it to understand it. I still don't today. People pay out a fortune to learn about it, but it's bullsh★★ – you either feel it or you don't.

I don't look at myself as a sexual singer and all that sh★★, but I can't control what people feel. I appreciate the accolades I receive. They say I'm the King of Romance, King of Love, but at the end of the day I'm just the king of my family, king of my own life.

In the evening, I might watch a movie. I have a wide-screen TV, black sofas and leopardskin chairs. Then I might sit and look at the sky. The sun is out there every day, and the stars and the moon are out there every night. It makes you realise you gotta appreciate what's real in life. **Barry White had a massive stroke in 2002. He died of kidney failure in July 2003, aged 58.**

# INDEX AND ACKNOWLEDGMENTS

With special thanks to the
editors of A Life in the Day:
Susan Raven 1977-1991
Hannah Charlton 1991-1993
Hilary Stafford-Clark 1993 onwar

Ali, **Muhammad** by Glenn Gale; photograph: David Montgomery
**Almodóvar, Pedro** by Bridget Freer; photograph: Catherine Cabrol
**Anderson, Pamela** by Garth Pearce; photograph: Phil Ramey
**Archer, Jeffrey** by Susan Raven; photograph: Tim O'Sullivan
**Bailey, Kimberley** by Caroline Scott; photograph: Pal Hansen
**Baker, Tom** by Jeffrey Bernard; photograph: Kenneth Griffiths
**Barry, Marc** by Marcelle Katz; photograph: Sacha Waldman
**Beckett, Sister Wendy** by Sue Fox; photograph: Justin Pumfrey
**Bernard, Jeffrey** by Ginny Dougary **Big Daddy** by Gail Curtis;
photograph: Red Saunders **Biggs, Ronnie** by Brian Moynahan;
photograph: Snowdon/Camera Press **Bird, Dickie** by Richard Johnson;
photograph: Tim MacPherson **Blunkett, David** by Moira Martingale;
photograph: Roger Scruton **Boy George** by Elizabeth Winkler;
photograph: Julian Broad/Katz Pictures **Branson, Richard** by
Richard Johnson **Brooks, Garth** by Simon Witter; photograph:
Paul Harris **Caine, Michael** by George Perry **Calment, Jeanne** by
Marcelle Katz; photograph: Roberto Frankenberg **Camaj, Roko** by
Marcelle Katz; photograph: David Drebin **Cartland, Barbara** by
Alison Miller **Chau, Kai Bong** by Caroline Scott; photograph:
Richard Jones/Sinopix/Rex **Cook, Beryl** by Ann McFerran **Cook, Peter**
by Lesley Cunliffe; photograph: Toby Glanville **Cooper, Alice** by
Danny Scott; photograph: Steve Labadessa **Cooper, Lady Diana** by
Jane McKerron **Cresswell, Janet** by Janet Cresswell **Dalai Lama** by
Vanya Kewley; photograph: Vanya Kewley **Dench, Judi** by Sue Fox;
photograph: Clive Boursnell **Feltz, Vanessa** by Ann McFerran;
photograph: Bill Robinson **Frodo** by Caroline Scott; photograph:
Jane Hilton **Gadaffi, Colonel Muammar** by Vanya Kewley
**Gerwat, Michael** by Caroline Scott; photograph: James Ross
**Glitter, Gary** by Nicki Household; photograph: Christine Hanscombe
**Gormley, Antony** by Ann McFerran; photograph: Tim MacPherson
**Grant, Cary** by Pauline Peters; photograph: Roger Perry
**Green, Stanley** by Charles Clasen; photograph: David Lavender
**Guy the Gorilla** by Hunter Davies; photograph: David Reed
**Hady, Dr Tariq Abbas** by Tom Stoddart; photograph: Tom Stoddart/
IPG **Hall, Jerry** by Gail Curtis; photograph: Jean Pigozzi
**Harpwood, Diane** by Diane Harpwood, **Harris, Mark** by
Caroline Scott; photograph: Luke Foreman **Harty, Russell** by
Jane McKerron; photograph: Red Saunders **Harvey, Daniel** by
Daniel Harvey; photograph: David Partner **Helfgott, David** by
Hilary Stafford-Clark **Heseltine, Michael** by Muriel Bowen;
photograph: Roger Perry **Hirst, Damien** by Richard Johnson;
photograph: Paul Massey **Husain, Princess Shahnaz** by
Cathy Scott-Clark and Adrian Levy; photograph: Dayanita Singh/NB
Pictures **Jagger, Bianca** by Georgina Montagu; photograph:
Harriet Logan/Network **Jones, Vinnie** by Danny Scott; photograph:
Greg Williams **Kent, Princess Michael of** by HRH Princess Michael
of Kent; photograph: Richard Dudley-Smith **Khan, Imran** by
Angela Wilkes; **Khatum, Monara** by Vanya Kewley; photograph:
Vanya Kewley **Lacroix, Christian** by Lailan Young; photograph:
Julio Donoso/Corbis **Leary, Timothy** by Steven Goldman; photograph:
Johnny Rozsa **Little Richard** by Richard Johnson **Mandela, Nelson** by

Marcelle Katz; photograph: Jillian Edelstein/Network
**McCann, Dorinda** by Dorinda McCann; photograph: Jane Hilton
**McCartney, Linda** by Glenn Gale **McLaren, Malcolm** by
Hannah Charlton; photograph: Victor Watts **McCourt, Frank** by
Sue Fox **McCririck, John** by Richard Johnson; photograph:
Mitch Jenkins **Miller, Arthur** by Caroline Scott and
Alexandra Lautenbacher; photograph: Inge Morath/Magnum
**Milligan, Spike** by Derek Hall **Monaco, Princess Grace of** by
David Taylor; photograph: Udo Schreiber/Katz Pictures **Moore, Patrick**
by Mike Durham **Morris, Johnny** by Richard Johnson; photograph:
Justin Quick **Nureyev, Rudolf** by Michele Jaffe; photograph:
Snowdon/Camera Press **Owen, Michael** by Bridget Freer; photograph:
Zed Nelson/IPG **Paddington Bear** by Michael Bond; reproduced by
permission of The Agency (London) Ltd © Michael Bond 1995. First
published by The Sunday Times Magazine. All rights reserved and
enquiries to The Agency (London) Ltd, 24 Pottery Lane, London W11
4LZ; Fax: 020 7727 9037 **Parton, Dolly** by Lauren St John;
photograph: Véronique Roland **Paterson, Jennifer** by Ann McFerran;
photograph: Sam Faulkner/NB Pictures **Pavarotti, Luciano** by
Lailan Young; photograph: Roger Perry **Payne, Cynthia** by
Veronica Groocock; photograph: David Lavender **Pearl, Mr** by
Marcelle Katz **Philpott, Mary** by Mary Philpott; photograph:
Roger Perry **Phuc, Phan Thi Kim** by Caroline Scott; photographs:
Jason Bell; Nick Ut/AP **Prescott, John** by Ann McFerran; photograph:
Mike Abrahams/Network **Ramsay, Gordon** by Richard Johnson;
photograph: Philip Sinden **Reeve, Christopher** by Kathy Brewis
**Richmond, Fiona** by Jane McKerron; photograph: Mike Abrahams/
Network **Ross, Philip** by Caroline Scott; photograph: Barry Lewis/
Network **Rowe, Baysee** by Caroline Scott; photograph: Anita Corbin
**Savile, Jimmy** by Glenn Gale; photograph: Don McCullin **Socks** by
Tony Barrell **Springer, Jerry** by Sue Fox **Starck, Philippe** by
Marcelle Katz; photograph: Jean-Baptiste Mondino **Sting** by
Danny Scott; photograph: Gigi Cohen/Network **Streeter, Tanya** by
Fiona Lafferty; photograph: Zena Holloway **Terre Blanche, Eugene** by
Marcelle Katz; photograph: Jillian Edelstein/Network **Tippett, Sir**
**Michael** by Ruth Hall **Toscani, Oliviero** by Marcelle Katz; photograph:
Guido Harari/Katz Pictures **Trump, Marla** by Marcelle Katz;
**Tuyisenge, Sophia Ingibire** by Ann McFerran; photograph:
Penny Tweedie **Ustinov, Peter** by David Taylor; photograph: Roger Perry
**Vegas, Johnny** by Ria Higgins; photograph: Muir Vidler **Warhol, Andy**
by Pauline Peters; photograph: Evelyn Hofer **Wax, Ruby** by Sue Fox;
photograph: Martin Dunkerton **Weston, Simon** by Susan King;
photograph: Clay Perry **White, Barry** by Ria Higgins; photograph:
Kevin Davies **Widdecombe, Ann** by Caroline Scott **Windsor, Barbara**
by Ria Higgins; photograph: Jane Hilton **Winslet, Kate** by Garth Pearce;
photograph: Sheila Rock **Wood, Victoria** by Eithne Power; photograph:
Iain McKell **Woodhouse, Barbara** by Ian Woodward **Zoya** by
John Follain and Rita Cristofari; photograph: Nick Cornish
**While all reasonable attempts have been made to contact**
**writers, photographers and copyright holders, this has**
**not proved possible in some cases**